Student Workbook

Entrepreneurship

Instructor's Annotated Workbook

Karel Sovak
Gary Tharaldson School of Business
University of Mary
Bismarck, North Dakota

Irina A. Weisblat, EdD
College of Business Administration
Trident University International
Cypress, California

Publisher
The Goodheart-Willcox Company, Inc.
Tinley Park, Illinois
www.g-w.com

Introduction

This workbook is designed for use with *Entrepreneurship*. Using this workbook will reinforce the concepts you learned in the text as well as provide enrichment activities to improve your communication skills.

Each chapter is organized into two parts: Check Your Knowledge and Activate Your Understanding. After reading the corresponding chapter in the text, complete as many exercises as you can without referring to the text. When you have completed the activities, then compare your answers to the information in the text to measure what you have learned.

The *Entrepreneurship* workbook is an effective self-assessment tool to prepare you for more formal assessment that your instructor may assign.

Copyright © 2013
by
The Goodheart-Willcox Company, Inc.

All rights reserved. No part of this work may be reproduced, stored, or transmitted in any form or by any electronic or mechanical means, including information storage and retrieval systems, without the prior written permission of The Goodheart-Willcox Company, Inc.

Manufactured in the United States of America.

ISBN 978-1-60525-784-6

1 2 3 4 5 6 7 8 9 – 12 – 17 16 15 14 13 12

Instructor's Annotated Workbook
ISBN 978-1-60525-905-5

1 2 3 4 5 6 7 8 9 – 12 – 17 16 15 14 13 12

Unit 1 Entrepreneurship...........................5

Chapter 1   Entrepreneurial Careers 5
Chapter 2   Business Plan 13
Chapter 3   Ethics and Social Responsibility 19

Unit 2 Explore the Opportunities 25

Chapter 4   Local and Global Opportunities.....................25
Chapter 5   Market Research 31
Chapter 6   Business Ownership 39

Unit 3 Building the Business........................47

Chapter 7   Site Selection 47
Chapter 8   Legal Issues 55
Chapter 9   Business Funding 61

Unit 4 Examining the Four Ps of Marketing...........67

Chapter 10 Product, Price, and Place 67
Chapter 11 Promotion and Selling 73
Chapter 12 Marketing Plan 79

Unit 5 Managing the Business 85

Chapter 13 Management Functions..............................85
Chapter 14 Human Resources Management 93
Chapter 15 Purchases and Inventory Management............101
Chapter 16 Risk Management 107
Chapter 17 Financial Management 115

Unit 6 Expanding and Exiting 121

Chapter 18 Business Growth....................................121
Chapter 19 Exit Strategies 127

Copyright Goodheart-Willcox Co., Inc.

Name _____ Date _____ Period _____

CHAPTER 1
Entrepreneurial Careers

Part 1: Check Your Knowledge

Multiple Choice

Write the letter of the correct answer to each question on the line provided.

__B__ 1. An entrepreneur is a person who
   A. provides funding for businesses.
   B. starts a new business.
   C. works for a major corporation.
   D. is looking for a new job.

__C__ 2. When following the problem-solving process to select a career, which of the following is the *first* step you might take?
   A. Write down all the career opportunities that fit your interests
   B. Enroll in courses that will help you in your career
   C. Select a career path
   D. Find a career that would provide the lifestyle you want

__B__ 3. The natural ability to do or learn something is a(n)
   A. attitude.
   B. aptitude.
   C. skill.
   D. goal.

__A__ 4. Which of the following characteristics is *least* important to the success of an entrepreneur?
   A. Good physical appearance
   B. Good leadership skills
   C. An aptitude for the chosen business
   D. A good attitude

__D__ 5. Another term for "people skills" is
   A. leadership skills.
   B. problem-solving skills.
   C. business skills.
   D. interpersonal skills.

__A__ 6. The behavioral and emotional characteristics that make each person unique are known as
   A. traits.
   B. skills.
   C. goals.
   D. leadership.

__B__ 7. To understand your own personal preferences and your strengths and weaknesses, you can complete a(n)
   A. career plan.
   B. self-assessment.
   C. employment application.
   D. portfolio.

__C__ 8. An experienced person who provides free advice and guidance to help an entrepreneur start a business is a(n)
   A. leader.
   B. customer.
   C. mentor.
   D. employer.

__A__ 9. A start-up business is one that
   A. is newly created.
   B. sells engine parts.
   C. branches off from a corporation.
   D. closes temporarily, then reopens.

__D__ 10. Which of the following is *not* a characteristic of a small business?
   A. Independently owned and operated
   B. Not dominant in its field
   C. Organized for profit
   D. Government-funded

True or False

On the line next to each of the following statements, write *True* if the statement is true, or write *False* if the statement is not true.

__True__ 11. Entrepreneurship is taking on the risks and responsibilities of a new business.

__False__ 12. Newly created companies are called *newbies*.

__False__ 13. SMART is an acronym for Strategic, Measurable, Attainable, Relevant and Time-oriented.

__False__ 14. Attitudes are the beliefs of a person or culture.

__True__ 15. Bill Gates and Oprah Winfrey are considered to be entrepreneurs.

__True__ 16. The word *entrepreneur* comes from the French word meaning "to undertake."

__True__ 17. Approximately 99 percent of all employers in the United States are considered small businesses.

__False__ 18. An aptitude is an ability a person has learned over time and can do well.

Chapter 1 Entrepreneurial Careers   **7**

Name _____

__True_____ 19. A leader empowers other people to act and make decisions.

__False_____ 20. Entrepreneurs need business skills only if they plan to start an accounting business.

Open Response

Write your response to each of the following statements or questions in the space provided.

21. Describe the SMART goal process. _____

    The SMART goal process is a method to define **S**pecific, **M**easurable, **A**ttainable, **R**ealistic, and

    Timely goals.

22. Which step in the SMART goal process is most often forgotten, and why is it important?

    The "Timely" step is most often overlooked. However, it is important to set an end date to keep

    progress on track and to help you remain motivated to meet the goal.

23. What is the difference between a skill and an aptitude? _____

    An aptitude is a natural ability to do or learn things. A skill, on the other hand, is something a

    person consciously takes steps to learn over a period of time.

24. List the seven steps of the problem-solving process. _____

    1. Define the challenge. 2. Analyze the situation. 3. Gather the facts. 4. Generate ideas.

    5. Consider the alternatives. 6. Make a decision. 7. Implement your decision.

25. List three types of fees that credit card companies may charge their customers.

    Student answers will vary. Common fees include annual fees, late payment fees, and over-limit

    fees.

26. What are the three main duties of a trustee when settling an estate?
The three main duties of a trustee are to pay off the debts of the estate, manage the assets until the estate is settled, and prepare and file tax returns.

27. What five types of skills must any good leader have?
Interpersonal skills, problem-solving skills, business skills, planning skills, and leadership skills

28. Name four basic skills that successful entrepreneurs need.
(any four) Reading, writing, listening, speaking, math

29. List four business skills that successful entrepreneurs should have.
(any four) Planning, organizing, negotiating, leadership, communication

30. What five personality traits do entrepreneurs need?
Passion, perseverance, persistence, planning, and problem solving

Chapter 1 Entrepreneurial Careers

Name _____

Part 2: Activate Your Understanding

Career Activities

Follow the directions provided for each activity. If necessary, write your response in the space provided.

1. Practice using the Career Clusters to focus your career search by performing the following steps.

   A. Take 3 to 5 minutes to brainstorm ideas about your future career path. Write down your initial ideas in the space below, as you think of them, in any order. Remember, your ideas are not limited to words. If a picture will better describe the concept, be sure to include it in the space provided below.

   > Student answers will vary.

B. Select three ideas that seem most appealing to you and write them in the first column of the table below.

C. Match your ideas with the possible career opportunities that you think may be appropriate. Write these in the second column.

D. Take a look at the Career Clusters described in textbook Figure 1-2 and see which of the Career Clusters each career opportunity fits in best. Write the name of a Career Cluster in the third column next to each career opportunity.

E. Finally, review the specific positions available within the Career Clusters you listed in the table. In the fourth column of the table, list a position in each Career Cluster that interests you or to which you can relate.

	Ideas	Possible Career Opportunity	Career Cluster	Interesting Position within Career Cluster
1.	Student answers will vary, but the Career Clusters in the third column should be related to the ideas and possible career opportunities in the first two columns, and the positions listed in the fourth column should relate to the Career Clusters listed in the third column.			
2.				
3.				

2. Brainstorm the careers you would like to pursue. Try to be creative, looking to combine different Career Clusters and possibly create a job that doesn't even exist today. In the first column of the table below, list five career ideas. In the second column, list the aptitudes you will need to have in order to pursue that career. In the third column, list the skills you will need to learn.

Career Idea	Aptitudes Needed	Skills Needed
Student answers will vary.		

Chapter 1 Entrepreneurial Careers 11

Name _____

3. The purpose of this exercise is for you to outline a career plan as an entrepreneur. Brainstorming business ideas and assessing your personal qualities are helpful in career planning. The table below outlines a career plan. In the first row, briefly describe an idea for a start-up business that interests you. The first column lists some important components of career planning. In the second column, write examples and details that best match your personal characteristics as an entrepreneur.

Components of a Career Plan	Student answers will vary.
Business Idea:	
	Examples and Details
Funding Sources for Your Business	
Aptitudes	
Attitudes	
Skills	
Business-Related Education	

4. Using the examples and details you entered in the table above, describe your career plan in a narrative format. Write a short three-paragraph essay in the blank space provided below. Your last paragraph should be a summary of what you expect to accomplish in the next five years. Be specific.

Entrepreneurship Career Plan

Student narratives will vary.

_____
_____
_____
_____
_____
_____
_____
_____
_____
_____
_____
_____
_____

5. Identify a career choice based on your work in the previous activities. (Remember, you can always change your choice later.) In the table below, list five SMART goals that would help you prepare for this career. Review each goal to make sure it meets all five requirements of the SMART goal process. Place a check mark in the appropriate columns after checking each requirement for each goal.

Goal	Specific	Measurable	Attainable	Realistic	Timely
1. Student answers will vary.					
2.					
3.					
4.					
5.					

6. Prepare for an interview with an entrepreneur. Develop a list of five interview questions you would ask in order to determine the aptitudes, attitudes, skills, and values necessary to become an entrepreneur. In your questions, use the vocabulary from this chapter.

Interview questions:

1. Student answers will vary.
2. _____
3. _____
4. _____
5. _____

7. Conduct an interview with an entrepreneur using the questions you prepared in the previous activity. During the interview, record or write down the entrepreneur's answers. After the interview, perform the following steps:

   A. Review your recording or notes, paying attention to key words that reveal the person's personality traits.
   B. Assess the entrepreneur's personality traits using the 5 Ps of personality traits for entrepreneurs.
   C. In the middle column of the table below, write a one-sentence summary of how well the entrepreneur meets each of the five traits.
   D. In the last column of the table, write a sentence evaluating your own personality traits as they relate to being an entrepreneur.

Personality Trait	Entrepreneur	Self
Passion	Student answers will vary.	
Perseverance		
Persistence		
Planning		
Problem Solving		

Name _____ Date _____ Period _____

CHAPTER 2: Business Plan

Part 1: Check Your Knowledge

Multiple Choice

Write the letter of the correct answer to each question on the line provided.

__B__ 1. According to the Small Business Administration, the percentage of businesses that survive the first five years is about
   A. 44%.
   B. 50%.
   C. 67%.
   D. 75%.

__C__ 2. Which of the following is *not* a common reason for failure of a new business?
   A. Insufficient start-up capital
   B. Lack of planning
   C. Overestimating the competition
   D. Unexpected growth

__A__ 3. The road map or course of action to be taken for a start-up business is described in the
   A. business plan.
   B. feasibility study.
   C. sales strategy.
   D. business license.

__C__ 4. Finding a need for a product or service on which to base a start-up business is the
   A. feasibility study.
   B. job search.
   C. discovery process.
   D. funding process.

__B__ 5. Which of the following items is classified as a need?
   A. Computer
   B. Food
   C. Vacation
   D. Cell phone

Copyright Goodheart-Willcox Co., Inc.

13

__D__ 6. An analysis that helps a person decide whether a new product or service idea is worth pursuing is a
   A. business strategy.
   B. financial overview.
   C. risk management evaluation.
   D. feasibility study.

__D__ 7. In which type of economy does the government determine what goods are produced, how much is produced, and the selling prices?
   A. Traditional economy
   B. Market economy
   C. Mixed economy
   D. Command economy

__A__ 8. Which of the following types of resources is *not* a factor of production?
   A. Consumer resources
   B. Capital resources
   C. Natural resources
   D. Human resources

__C__ 9. The four basic market structures are oligopoly, monopoly, monopolistic competition, and
   A. imperfect competition.
   B. imperfect monopoly.
   C. perfect competition.
   D. perfect oligopoly.

__B__ 10. The part of a business plan that explains how the business will function if an unexpected event occurs is a
   A. financial plan.
   B. contingency plan.
   C. vision statement.
   D. risk management plan.

True or False

On the line next to each of the following statements, write *True* if the statement is true, or write *False* if the statement is not true.

__False__ 11. To be considered an entrepreneur, you must invent a new product or service.

__True__ 12. Every new venture has some sort of risk associated with it.

__False__ 13. A smartphone is an example of a consumer need.

__True__ 14. The location of a business may cause the business to fail.

__True__ 15. Start-up money is also called *seed money*.

__False__ 16. A pro forma financial statement is a final financial statement made after all of the year's financial statistics have been verified.

__True__ 17. A market evaluation should include an analysis of the opportunity for growth in the industry.

__False__ 18. If a product idea is good enough, the amount of competition does not need to be considered.

Chapter 2   Business Plan

Name _____

___False___ 19. A mission statement should be developed from the entrepreneur's perspective.

___False___ 20. A good business plan does not need updating after the business has opened.

Matching

Read the numbered definitions of parts of a business plan. Then, choose the correct term from the list that follows and write the letter on the line provided next to the definition.

___I___ 21. Informs the reader of where each section of the plan is located.

___E___ 22. Provides an overview of the business.

___C___ 23. Includes a description of the product or service, goals, mission and vision statements, and proposed location.

___H___ 24. Describes the organizational structure of the business and the management team.

___A___ 25. Includes documents to support the plan, such as résumés and financial statements.

___F___ 26. Describes start-up capital and sources of funds.

___J___ 27. Presents the name of the company, the owner, and the date the plan is presented.

___B___ 28. Lists the resources that were used to develop the business plan.

___D___ 29. Summarizes why the business will be successful and requests financing.

___G___ 30. Describes industry conditions, economic conditions, and competition, and specifies the target market.

A. appendices
B. bibliography
C. business description
D. conclusion
E. executive summary
F. financial plan
G. market evaluation
H. operations
I. table of contents
J. title page

Part 2: Activate Your Understanding

Chapter Activities

1. Feasibility Study

   A. Working with a partner, brainstorm ideas for a start-up business. Hobbies are an excellent source of idea generation. For example, you may wish to consider opening a comic book store, or start a game center. Write your ideas on the lines below. Generate as many ideas as possible.

   Student ideas will vary.

   _____
   _____
   _____
   _____

B. With your partner, select one of the ideas you listed and conduct a feasibility study on it. Your research should include finding statistics about the industry. For example, how much would it cost to start this business? What is the best location for the business? Who will your customers be? Conduct a survey of potential customers to find out if they would buy your product or service. Record the idea you selected and the results of your research in the space provided.

Idea for feasibility study: <u>Student answers will vary.</u>

C. Is this idea feasible? Write your recommendation for or against this idea in the space provided, and explain why you think the idea is or is not feasible.

Student answers will vary.

2. Business Plan Review

   A. Obtain a business plan from an existing small business in your community. Write the name of the business in the space provided.

   Business plan for: _____

   B. Compare and contrast the executive summary in the business plan to the actual business operations to determine how well the summary reflects the way the business is being run. Write your observations in the space provided.

   Student answers will vary.

Chapter 2   Business Plan

Name _____

C. Carefully review each section of the plan and compare its contents with the business plan template in this chapter. Write a short analysis of each business plan section listed in the table below.

Section	Analysis
Executive Summary	Student answers will vary.
Business Description	
Market Evaluation	
Operations	
Financial Plans	

Communication Activities

3. You and a friend are thinking about opening a new café-style restaurant that caters to the lunchtime needs of area businesses. Conduct research to find sources of start-up money available in your area. Prepare a sources of funds document to include in the Financial Plans section of your business plan. In the space provided, list the sources you used to gather the information and prepare your document.

   Student answers will vary.

4. Consider the advantages and disadvantages of purchasing a franchise instead of opening an independent start-up business. Record your thoughts in the table below. Decide which option you would prefer. Then prepare a persuasive speech to convince your classmates that purchasing a franchise is or is not a better idea than opening an independent business.

Advantages of Franchise	Disadvantages of Franchise
Student answers will vary.	

5. Find a business that is for sale in your community. Conduct research to find out why the business is for sale, and whether it is in good financial condition. Write a report explaining why this would or would not be a good business opportunity for an entrepreneur. In the space provided, record the name of the business you researched and the sources you used to investigate it.

   Student answers will vary.

6. You are considering starting a business to sell customized greeting cards. Analyze the competition. In the space provided, list the leading competitors. Then create an executive summary for your business plan that outlines ideas to make your cards different or better than the competition.

   Student answers will vary.

CHAPTER 3: Ethics and Social Responsibility

Part 1: Check Your Knowledge

Multiple Choice

Write the letter of the correct answer to each question on the line provided.

__C__ 1. A set of general guidelines outlining the acceptable behavior from a company when dealing with customers, vendors, and fellow employees is a
   A. confidentiality agreement.
   B. code of conduct.
   C. code of ethics.
   D. conflict of interest.

__C__ 2. Individuals' medical records are protected under the federal
   A. code of conduct.
   B. intellectual property laws.
   C. HIPAA Privacy Rule.
   D. Environmental Protection Agency.

__B__ 3. The term *trade secrets* refers to a company's
   A. insider trading.
   B. proprietary information.
   C. corporate social responsibility.
   D. philanthropy.

__D__ 4. A form potential employees may be required to sign agreeing not to share company information with outsiders is a(n)
   A. code of ethics.
   B. vision statement.
   C. intellectual property statement.
   D. confidentiality agreement.

__A__ 5. A protection typically obtained for music, paintings, and other original work to prevent others from stealing a person's creation is a
   A. copyright.
   B. plagiarism.
   C. confidentiality agreement.
   D. trademark.

__C__ 6. The belief that an organization has an obligation to society that goes beyond simply making money is known as
   A. a code of ethics.
   B. infringement.
   C. social responsibility.
   D. plagiarism.

__A__ 7. The agency that provides information to companies about the environment and environmentally responsible behaviors is
   A. EPA.
   B. HIPAA.
   C. OSHA.
   D. FCC.

__B__ 8. Using copyrighted information without giving credit to or obtaining permission from the author or creator is known as
   A. infringement.
   B. plagiarism.
   C. patent violation.
   D. insider trading.

__D__ 9. Rules of behavior based on ideas about what is right and wrong are
   A. goodwill.
   B. philanthropy.
   C. copyright.
   D. ethics.

__C__ 10. A sign an inventor has obtained for a product or service that indicates that it belongs to the inventor is called a(n)
   A. ethical agreement.
   B. patent violation.
   C. trademark.
   D. infringement.

True or False

On the line next to each of the following statements, write *True* if the statement is true, or write *False* if the statement is not true.

__False__ 11. Using copyrighted material without giving the author credit is illegal, but it is not unethical.

__False__ 12. Social responsibility is the belief that a company has to maximize its profits in order to be a good community provider.

__False__ 13. Using copyrighted material without permission is known as infringement.

__True__ 14. Any employee action that divides the employee's loyalty between the company and an outside endeavor is considered a conflict of interest.

__False__ 15. As long as a company is not breaking laws, it is being ethical.

__True__ 16. Insider trading is both unethical and illegal.

__False__ 17. A company must comply with local and state laws only if those laws do not conflict with the company's code of ethics.

Chapter 3   Ethics and Social Responsibility

Name _____

__True_____ 18. Freeware is software that is available for no charge.

__True_____ 19. Malware is software that contains a computer virus or other harmful code designed to damage a computer.

__True_____ 20. One way a company can help the environment is to use green products.

Matching

Read the numbered definitions. Then, choose the correct term from the list that follows and write the letter on the line provided next to the definition.

__D__ 21. Software available at no charge that can be used at any time.

__A__ 22. A list of acceptable behavior for specific business situations.

__H__ 23. Using someone else's words without giving credit to the person who wrote them.

__C__ 24. How a company's owners and employees think, feel, and act as a business.

__B__ 25. Statement of general principles or values that guide an organization.

__I__ 26. Copyrighted software that is available free of charge on a trial basis.

__E__ 27. The advantage a business has due to its good reputation.

__G__ 28. Promoting the welfare of others.

__J__ 29. Behaving with sensitivity to social, economic, and environmental issues.

__F__ 30. An employee uses private company information to purchase stock or securities for personal gain.

A. code of conduct
B. code of ethics
C. corporate culture
D. freeware
E. goodwill
F. insider trading
G. philanthropy
H. plagiarism
I. shareware
J. socially responsible

Part 2: Activate Your Understanding

Chapter Activities

1. Conflict of Interest

   Read each of the following scenarios and determine whether a conflict of interest exists. In the space provided, explain why you believe a conflict of interest does or does not exist.

   A. Jamil works in a store that sells athletic equipment and supplies. His sales record is good, because Jamil offers potential customers private lessons after hours on how to use the equipment. He charges $35 per session. The company is aware that Jamil is offering this service, and has expressed its approval.

   Student answers will vary. If Jamil had been making these offers without the company's knowledge, a conflict of interest might be assumed. However, since the company knows and approves, Jamil is probably not doing anything unethical. In fact, even though he makes money on the side, his offer of instruction may help the company sell more exercise equipment.

   B. Angela works at a cosmetics counter in a department store. At night, she operates a small company selling cut-rate cosmetics. When a department store customer complains that the prices of the store's cosmetics are too high, Angela quietly gives the customer her business card and tells the customer to call her later for a better deal.

   This is a definite conflict of interest. Angela's company is in direct competition with her employer, and she is taking business away from her employer.

   C. Denny has a daytime job assembling parts at a manufacturing plant. At night, he sells real estate to help make ends meet.

   This is not a conflict of interest. The real estate work has no impact on the manufacturing company, or vice versa, as long as Denny does not use knowledge gained at one job to help the other job at the first job's expense.

Chapter 3 Ethics and Social Responsibility

Name _____

2. Green Company

Choose a small business in your area and ask the owner's permission to analyze the company's environmental practices. Explain that you will provide a list of ideas, tailored to the business, to help make the company "greener." After obtaining permission, analyze the company's business practices. In the space provided, write the name of the company and list ideas to help the company reduce wastes, recycle, and re-use items it is currently discarding. Make the list available to the business owner.

Name of company: _____

Green ideas: _Student answers will vary._____

_____

_____

_____

_____

_____

_____

3. Code of Ethics vs. Code of Conduct

Read each of the statements below and determine whether it is more likely from a company's code of ethics or code of conduct. Place each statement in the correct column in the table below.

A. Treat customers the way you would like to be treated.

B. Do not accept gifts from vendors.

C. If a customer leaves a message for you to call, return the call promptly.

D. This company depends on the honesty and integrity of its employees.

E. When dining with a customer, do not drink alcoholic beverages.

Code of Ethics	Code of Conduct
Answers may vary, because some of these items may be included in either a code of ethics or a code of conduct. Suggested answers: code of ethics: A, D; code of conduct: B, C, and E.	

Communication Activities

4. Choose a type of business that you would like to start. Think about the ethical issues that might arise as you run this particular type of business. List at least three issues in the space provided. Then prepare a written report describing how you would deal with each of the issues you listed.

    Type of business: __Student answers will vary.__

    Possible ethical issues: _____

    _____

    _____

    _____

5. Choose a shareware program that you have used or that you would like to try. Read the rules regarding how long the shareware may be used before buying it. Also determine whether the shareware version is fully functional or a less capable version of the actual software. Write an informative report explaining how this company's shareware does or does not help increase software sales. In the space provided, record the name of the shareware program and write a one-sentence summary of what you have learned.

    Shareware name: __Student answers will vary.__

    Summary: _____

    _____

6. Interview someone in the IT department of a local company. Ask about the company's guidelines for downloading software onto company computers. Find out the reasons for the guidelines. Prepare an oral report to explain your findings to the class. In the space provided, record the name of the company and the person you interviewed.

    Student answers will vary.

    _____

    _____

7. Choose a large company that is often in the news, such as one of the large oil companies or a financial company. Conduct research to determine what philanthropic projects the company is currently undertaking. Write an analytical report describing how these particular projects may help both the recipients and the company. In the space provided, record the name of the company and list the philanthropic projects.

    Company: __Student answers will vary__

    Projects: _____

    _____

    _____

    _____

Chapter 4: Local and Global Opportunities

Part 1: Check Your Knowledge

Multiple Choice

Write the letter of the correct answer to each question on the line provided.

__A__ 1. Which of the following organizations promotes the commercial interests of a community and consists of small business owners, entrepreneurs, government leaders, and other interested individuals?
A. Chamber of commerce
B. Small business development corporation
C. Better Business Bureau
D. Conflict of interest

__A__ 2. Depressed communities that receive special tax credits and other incentives to stimulate business are known as
A. enterprise zones.
B. service organizations.
C. joint ventures.
D. importers.

__B__ 3. The SBA considers for-profit companies that are independently owned and operated and are not dominant in their field to be
A. service organizations.
B. small businesses.
C. joint ventures.
D. enterprise zones.

__D__ 4. People from all countries use both verbal and nonverbal forms of
A. licensing.
B. vision statement.
C. logistics.
D. communication.

__C__ 5. A shipping company that transports goods from a manufacturer to a retail store is considered part of a(n)
   A. exchange rate.
   B. enterprise zone.
   C. supply chain.
   D. tariff.

__B__ 6. Which of the following is a nonprofit organization made up of retired executives who volunteer to provide one-on-one mentoring?
   A. BBB
   B. SCORE
   C. SBDC
   D. SBA

__D__ 7. Rather than manufacturing a product or providing a service, an entrepreneur may decide to go into business through
   A. communication.
   B. tariffs.
   C. tax authorities.
   D. licensing.

__C__ 8. To sell your product in a country that does not allow foreign-owned businesses, you could work with a local business through a
   A. tariff.
   B. free enterprise system.
   C. joint venture.
   D. local university.

__A__ 9. If you plan to ship goods to another country and do not understand international shipping regulations, you may need to hire a company that specializes in international shipping
   A. logistics.
   B. licensing.
   C. ethics.
   D. exchange rates.

__B__ 10. To find global buyers, many US businesses use
   A. export trading companies.
   B. export management companies.
   C. licensors.
   D. interpreters.

True or False

On the line next to each of the following statements, write *True* if the statement is true, or write *False* if the statement is not true.

__True__ 11. Small businesses help the economy by keeping production and manufacturing in the United States.

__False__ 12. The SBA provides services such as reliability reports to both businesses and consumers.

__True__ 13. The purpose of an enterprise zone is to stimulate local economies.

__False__ 14. The small business development center is administered by SCORE.

Chapter 4 Local and Global Opportunities

Name _____

__True_____ 15. An entrepreneur doing business globally must understand cultural differences to avoid offending people in other countries.

__False_____ 16. Exchange rates are updated monthly.

__True_____ 17. A person who buys a license to use a trademark is known as the licensee.

__True_____ 18. In a joint venture between two companies, the companies remain independent.

__False_____ 19. NAFTA is an example of a tariff.

__True_____ 20. The United States has laws that prohibit importing products from countries that abuse human rights.

Matching

Read the numbered definitions. Then, choose the correct term from the list that follows and write the letter on the line provided next to the definition.

__H__ 21. The businesses, people, and activities involved in turning raw materials into products and delivering them to end users.

__C__ 22. Shipping products made in one country to another country for future sale.

__A__ 23. Nonprofit organization established in 1912 to evaluate and monitor businesses.

__E__ 24. Planning and managing the flow of goods, services, and people to a destination.

__I__ 25. A tax on imported goods.

__F__ 26. Nonprofit organization that provides one-on-one mentoring by retired business executives.

__B__ 27. The rate at which one currency can be converted to another.

__G__ 28. Government agency that provides online and face-to-face assistance to small businesses and entrepreneurs.

__D__ 29. Bringing products made in one country into another country for future sale.

__J__ 30. A governmental regulation that restricts trade with other countries.

A. Better Business Bureau
B. exchange rate
C. exporting
D. importing
E. logistics
F. SCORE
G. Small Business Administration
H. supply chain
I. tariff
J. trade barrier

Part 2: Activate Your Understanding

Chapter Activities

1. SCORE

    Locate the SCORE chapter that serves your community and find out more about how it supports small businesses and entrepreneurs in your community.

    A. What cities and towns does the chapter serve?
    Student answers will vary.

    B. What services does this chapter offer?
    Student answers will vary. Many chapters offer direct help with tax issues, as well as individual business counseling and free workshops to help small businesses and entrepreneurs succeed.

    C. List five questions that you would like to ask a SCORE counselor.
    1. Student answers will vary.
    2.
    3.
    4.
    5.

2. Better Business Bureau

    Conduct research through the Better Business Bureau. Search for information on each of the following businesses in your area. List the top three companies in each category and summarize the review of each.

    A. Plumbers
    1. Student answers will vary.
    2.
    3.

Chapter 4   Local and Global Opportunities

Name _____

　B. Electricians

　　1. Student answers will vary.

　　2.

　　3.

　C. Bakeries

　　1. Student answers will vary.

　　2.

　　3.

3. Small Business Administration

Conduct research to find out more about the activities and resources available through the Small Business Administration.

　A. In addition to helping entrepreneurs start a business, what other services does the national SBA offer?

　　Student answers will vary. Other services include helping small businesses get loans, helping them navigate government contracts, and providing disaster assistance, including SBA disaster loans.

　B. What is SBA Direct?

　　SBA direct is a web-based tool that allows users to find the resources they need in their local area. Users answer questions about their business needs, and the tool provides targeted information in response.

4. Exchange Rate

   Choose three countries in which you would like to conduct business. Compare the currency exchange rate with the US dollar for each country. Record your findings in the table below. Of the three countries, which would be the most favorable place to start a business? Record your answer in the space provided.

Country	Exchange Rate
Student answers will vary depending on the countries they choose and the current exchange rates.	

   Most favorable place to start a business: _____

Communication Activities

5. Conduct research to find the meaning of the terms *balance of trade* and *trade deficit*, and write the definitions in the space provided. Then write an informative report explaining the current status of the United States.

   Balance of trade: _____The balance of trade is the difference in value between a country's total imports and total exports._____

   Trade deficit: _____A trade deficit is the amount by which a country's imports exceed its exports._____
   Student reports will vary, but in 2011, the US trade deficit was $558 billion.

6. Conduct research to find out more about free trade agreements. With what countries does the United States currently have free trade agreements? Record the countries in the space provided. Then prepare an informative report explaining how the agreements affect US trade with these countries.

   Countries: _____
   The US currently has 12 free trade agreements that affect 17 countries: Australia, Bahrain, Chile, Costa Rica, Dominican Republic, El Salvador, Guatemala, Honduras, Nicaragua, Israel, Jordan, Morocco, Canada, Mexico, Oman, Peru, and Singapore.

7. Interview someone at your local chamber of commerce. Prepare an oral report to explain your findings to the class.

   A. How does the chamber support entrepreneurs and small businesses in your area?
   Student answers will vary.

   B. What are the advantages of becoming a member of the chamber of commerce?
   Student answers will vary.

CHAPTER 5: Market Research

Part 1: Check Your Knowledge

Multiple Choice

Write the letter of the correct answer to each question on the line provided.

__C__ 1. A SWOT analysis is designed to help a company determine its
  A. sales, wages, overhead, and target.
  B. sales, wages, occupations, and trends.
  C. strengths, weaknesses, opportunities, and threats.
  D. strengths, weaknesses, overhead, and trends.

__D__ 2. Geographic segmentation is based on
  A. customers' lifestyles.
  B. customers' decision-making process.
  C. how much the customers earn.
  D. where the customers live.

__A__ 3. A detailed description of customers based on demographic, geographic, psychographic, and behavioral information is gathered to create a
  A. customer profile.
  B. target market.
  C. market segment.
  D. SWOT analysis.

__C__ 4. A target market is made up of
  A. retail stores in the domestic market.
  B. buyers in the foreign market.
  C. a group of customers.
  D. employees in the marketing department.

__B__ 5. All of the following items are psychographic segmentation variables *except*
  A. activities.
  B. occupations.
  C. attitudes.
  D. values.

__B__ 6. Secondary data are
   A. data collected by you or your organization.
   B. data that has already been collected by someone else.
   C. data that are more than five years old.
   D. data that have no relevance to your organization.

__C__ 7. Data mining involves uncovering trends by
   A. developing a research plan.
   B. studying the competition.
   C. analyzing information.
   D. stating a hypothesis.

__D__ 8. Which of the following questions would be *least* useful for defining the problem of starting a profitable business?
   A. Where should I locate the business?
   B. What products or services should I sell?
   C. What are the demographics of the potential customers?
   D. What color should I paint the office walls?

__B__ 9. An organized study in which all the participants are asked the same questions is a
   A. database.
   B. study.
   C. journal.
   D. research plan.

__A__ 10. The processes of collecting, analyzing, and reporting market research information make up a
   A. marketing information system.
   B. market segmentation.
   C. competitive analysis.
   D. mass market.

True or False

On the line next to each of the following statements, write *True* if the statement is true, or write *False* if the statement is not true.

__True__ 11. One type of competitive advantage is a special feature of your product that is not offered by the products of your competitors.

__True__ 12. Marital status is a factor that is considered in demographic segmentation.

__False__ 13. Education level does not appear to influence customer purchases.

__False__ 14. Primary data can be easily and cheaply obtained from the Internet, government databases, and other sources.

__False__ 15. Qualitative data are primary data that consist of facts and figures.

__True__ 16. Market research may not provide the right information if it is performed incorrectly.

__True__ 17. Trade associations are a good source of secondary data.

__False__ 18. The market segment in market research is the number of people in the group from which the data are collected.

Chapter 5 Market Research

Name _____

__True___ 19. Benefits are reasons a product will make customers' lives better.

__False__ 20. *Competitive analysis* is another term for a SWOT analysis.

Matching

Read the numbered definitions. Then, choose the correct term from the list that follows and write the letter on the line provided next to the definition.

__J__ 21. How often a customer buys or uses a product or service.

__A__ 22. Company that sells primarily to businesses.

__F__ 23. Statement that can be tested and proved true or false.

__D__ 24. Giving customers greater value, better products, or something not offered by the competition.

__C__ 25. A count of the people living in the country.

__I__ 26. Statement that lists a product's special features or benefits and highlights its advantages.

__G__ 27. Mathematical technique for analyzing data.

__B__ 28. Company that sells primarily to consumers.

__E__ 29. Organizing data and studying it to find useful trends or patterns.

__H__ 30. The specific group of customers at which a company aims its products or services.

A. B2B company
B. B2C company
C. census
D. competitive advantage
E. data analysis
F. hypothesis
G. statistical analysis
H. target market
I. unique selling proposition
J. usage rate

Part 2: Activate Your Understanding

Chapter Activities

1. Studying the Competition

    Choose a small business in your community that interests you. Pretend you are considering purchasing this business. One of the things you will need to know is how stiff the competition is. Identify two companies that are in direct competition with the business you chose. Fill in the following table to describe the strengths and weaknesses of your chosen business and its competitors.

Company Name	Strengths	Weaknesses
Name of the business you chose: Student answers will vary.		
Competitor 1:		
Competitor 2:		

2. Competitive Advantage

    Choose a type of product or service that you think you could provide successfully in your community. It can be an existing product or service or your own original idea.

    A. What name will you give your product or service?
    Student answers will vary.

    B. List at least two special features of this product or service and describe their associated benefits to customers.
    Student answers will vary, but students should demonstrate understanding of the difference between features and benefits.

    C. How would you price your product or service compared to the competition? Explain.
    Student answers will vary.

Chapter 5   Market Research

Name _____

D. Based on your answers to parts B and C, write a sentence to summarize your competitive edge.

Student answers will vary.

3. Focus Group

Ask a group of six to nine classmates to form a focus group to discuss the product or service you identified in question 2.

A. Prepare at least five questions to ask the members of the group, and record them in the space provided.

1. Student answers will vary.

2.

3.

4.

5.

B. Develop a chart or table in which you can easily record the answers of the focus group members. Conduct the focus group, and use your chart to record the answers from focus group members. In the space provided, describe the group's overall response to your product. Which features were popular? Which may need more work or development?

Student answers will vary.

4. Research Process

Suppose you have been thinking about starting a small computer repair business. Use the formal research process to narrow your options and decide whether such a business is feasible in your community. Record your results by filling in the right side of the following table.

Define the problem.	Student answers will vary.
Conduct background research. Summarize your results.	
State a hypothesis.	
Develop a research plan.	
Collect the data. List the actual sources of your data.	
Analyze the data. Summarize your analysis.	
Draw conclusions.	
Make recommendations.	

Chapter 5 Market Research

Name _____

Communication Activities

5. Identify a product that interests you. Identify the target market for this product by performing market segmentation. Record your results in the space provided. Then prepare an oral presentation to describe the target market for this product. In your presentation, explain how the market segmentation helped you define the target market.

   Geographic segmentation: *Student answers will vary.*
   _____
   _____

   Demographic segmentation: _____
   _____
   _____

   Psychographic segmentation: _____
   _____
   _____

   Behavioral segmentation: _____
   _____
   _____

6. Conduct research to find specific sources of secondary marketing data and how they can be accessed. In the space provided, list the resources you find, along with access information. Prepare a brochure to help entrepreneurs in your area locate and access these sources.

   Student answers will vary.
   _____
   _____
   _____
   _____

Chapter 6: Business Ownership

Part 1: Check Your Knowledge

Multiple Choice

Write the letter of the correct answer to each question on the line provided.

__D__ 1. The legal document that contains information a franchisee must know before purchasing a franchise and must be received by the buyer 14 days before an agreement is signed is the
   A. Franchise Rule Compliance Guide.
   B. uniform franchise offering circular.
   C. DBA license.
   D. franchise disclosure document.

__B__ 2. The company that sells the rights of a franchise is the
   A. franchisee.
   B. franchisor.
   C. host company.
   D. sponsor.

__B__ 3. Which of the following organizations regulates the franchising industry?
   A. Federal Trade Commission
   B. International Franchise Association
   C. Federal Communications Commission
   D. Small Business Administration

__A__ 4. A for-profit business that is owned and operated by a single person is known as a(n)
   A. sole proprietorship.
   B. C corporation.
   C. subchapter S corporation.
   D. partnership.

__C__ 5. A person who invests in a business but takes no part in the day-to-day operations of the business is called a(n)
   A. franchisee.
   B. franchisor.
   C. silent partner.
   D. entrepreneur.

__A__ 6. A partnership carries the risk of
   A. unlimited liability.
   B. limited start-up capital.
   C. double taxation.
   D. high start-up costs.

__D__ 7. A subchapter S corporation is designed to accommodate small businesses that have
   A. fewer than 50 employees.
   B. less than $5 million in revenue.
   C. more than 5 years of business experience.
   D. fewer than 100 stockholders.

__B__ 8. Which of the following is *not* an advantage of purchasing a franchise?
   A. Established image and brand
   B. Low start-up costs
   C. Training
   D. Financial advice

__D__ 9. One of the advantages of a family-owned business is
   A. easy financing.
   B. state-of-the-art equipment.
   C. conflicting interests.
   D. flexibility.

__C__ 10. In some states, a DBA license is known as a
   A. charter.
   B. partnership agreement.
   C. fictitious name registration.
   D. employer identification number.

True or False

On the line next to each of the following statements, write *True* if the statement is true, or write *False* if the statement is not true.

__False__ 11. The process of buying a franchise begins with the franchise disclosure document.

__True__ 12. Most franchises have strict rules of operation that must be followed by the franchisee.

__False__ 13. Buying an existing business eliminates the potential problem of reluctant partners.

__False__ 14. One advantage of joining a family-owned business is that conflicting interests are rarely a problem.

__True__ 15. A sole proprietor is personally responsible for all business debts.

__True__ 16. Businesses that hire employees must have an employer identification number assigned by the IRS.

__False__ 17. The tax benefits of a partnership are similar to those of a corporation.

__True__ 18. In a general partnership, all of the partners have unlimited liability.

Chapter 6 Business Ownership **41**

Name _____

<u>　True　</u>　19. A corporation is a legal entity.

<u>　False　</u>　20. A business must incorporate in a state where it is physically located.

Open Response

Write your response to each of the following statements or questions in the space provided.

21. Name four start-up strategies for businesses.

    Strategies include starting a new business, buying an existing business, purchasing a franchise, and joining a family business.

22. You are considering the purchase of a franchise for XYZ Snack Shops. What questions should you ask about the franchise before deciding to purchase it?

    You should investigate the franchisor and its record of performance and operation. Ask for the company's tax records and for information about management. Contact other franchisees and ask if their experience with the franchisor has been satisfactory.

23. Name four organizations that can provide resources on state, local, and national franchise laws.

    The FTC, IFA, SBA, and US Department of Commerce can provide these resources.

24. What start-up and ongoing costs are associated with buying a franchise?

    Costs include the initial franchise fee, grand opening fee, and royalty payments.

25. Name three disadvantages of buying an existing business.

    Disadvantages include expensive purchase price, if the business is prosperous; obsolete inventory, equipment, or processes; and reluctant partners.

Copyright Goodheart-Willcox Co., Inc.

26. What four things should you do before you sign a contract to buy or join a business?

    You should do your research, establish the value of the business, review the applicable laws, and get help from the professionals.

27. Name four benefits of being a sole proprietor.

    Benefits include being able to make all of the decisions; keeping all the profits for yourself; easy business start-up; and taxes that are lower than in many other types of businesses.

28. What does a partnership agreement specify?

    A partnership agreement details how much each partner will invest, each partner's responsibilities, and how profits are to be distributed.

29. What is a charter, and what form of business requires one?

    A charter, which is required for corporations, is a document that describes the purpose, place of business, and other details of a corporation.

30. What are the differences between a limited liability company and a limited liability partnership?

    The owners of an LLC are called members. LLCs can choose any organizational structure the members agree to, but they have a limited life—the business ends when one member retires, leaves the business, or dies. The owners of an LLP are called partners. The LLP has a similar business structure to a limited partnership (LP), but it has no managing partner. All of the partners have limited personal liability.

Chapter 6   Business Ownership

Name _____

Part 2: Activate Your Understanding

Chapter Activities

1. Researching Franchises

    Select two local franchises that interest you. Examples of franchises include Jiffy Lube®, Napa® Auto Parts, Subway®, and many other stores and restaurants that have locations all over the United States. Conduct research on the franchising requirements of each company. Complete the following table to record the initial fees, royalty payments, and any other information that might influence your decision to purchase the franchise. In the space provided below the table, indicate which of the two franchises you would prefer to purchase, and why.

Franchise Name	Initial Franchise Fees	Royalty Amount	Other Franchise Fees	Other Information

Student answers will vary.

2. International Franchise Association

   Conduct research to find out more about the International Franchise Association. Find the answers to the following questions.

   A. What is the purpose of the IFA's Diversity Institute?

   The Diversity Institute provides education, scholarships, and other resources to minority

   franchisees, as well as franchisees who are interested in expanding their diversity

   recruitment.

   B. What resources does the IFA provide to people who are looking for a franchise to purchase?

   The IFA has an easy-to-use searchable database that allows people to search for franchise

   opportunities by entering keywords, by category, or by initial investment amount.

   C. What is the name of the IFA's mentoring program?

   The IFA's mentoring program is called Franship.

3. Family-Owned Business Resources

   Many resources exist specifically to help family-owned businesses. Conduct research to find at least two resources that can help family-owned businesses with start-up, planning, and meeting on-going challenges. Record the resources in the space provided.

   Student answers will vary. Examples include documents available from the SBA, such as

   "Transferring Management in the Family-Owned Business,"; *Family Business* magazine; and

   efamilybusiness.com.

Communication Activities

4. Prepare a list of five questions that you would like to ask a business owner about conducting business as a sole proprietor. Record your questions in the space provided. Then obtain an appointment for an interview with a sole proprietor who owns a business in your area. Ask the questions you prepared and record the answers. Prepare an oral presentation of your findings to present to the class.

   Question 1: Student answers will vary.

   Question 2: _____

Chapter 6 Business Ownership

Name _____

Question 3: _____

_____

Question 4: _____

_____

Question 5: _____

_____

5. Meet with two classmates to consider establishing a new business as a partnership. Discuss the types of business you could start, and come to an agreement on a single business idea. Create a formal partnership agreement detailing how much each of you will invest, what responsibilities each person will have, and how much (what percentage) of the profit each partner will receive. Record your decisions in the table below. Then write a report describing any problems or disagreements that occurred and how you overcame them.

Name of Partner	Investment	Responsibilities	Percent Profit
Student answers will vary.			

6. Conduct research to find out more about starting a subchapter S corporation. Write an informative report explaining the requirements for starting the corporation. In the space provided, record the sources you used to form your report.

Reports will vary. The company must be a domestic corporation, and none of the shareholders can be partnerships or nonresident aliens. The corporation must have no more than 100 shareholders and can only have one class of stock.

Chapter 7: Site Selection

Part 1: Check Your Knowledge

Multiple Choice

Write the letter of the correct answer to each question on the line provided.

__B__ 1. The types of businesses that can operate in a community are regulated by local
   A. community incentives.
   B. zoning laws.
   C. chamber of commerce members.
   D. economic indicators.

__A__ 2. The link that distributes a product from a supplier to the consumer is a(n)
   A. supply chain.
   B. shipping center.
   C. employee chain.
   D. office hub.

__D__ 3. Brick-and-mortar businesses are those that
   A. manufacture construction products.
   B. have at least one brick wall.
   C. design custom homes.
   D. operate from a specific physical location.

__B__ 4. Businesses that blend physical locations and other distribution methods, such as an e-business that uses a brick-and-mortar warehouse, are
   A. joint ventures.
   B. hybrid businesses.
   C. foreign ventures.
   D. facilitated businesses.

__C__ 5. A legal agreement used to rent property or space from another person or company is a
   A. purchase agreement.
   B. franchise.
   C. lease.
   D. product license.

__D__ 6. The area from which a business expects to draw most of its customers is the
  A. target market.
  B. floor plan.
  C. enterprise zone.
  D. trade area.

__A__ 7. Which of the following is *not* an advantage of a home-based business?
  A. Reduced need to focus
  B. Lower overhead
  C. Freedom to schedule hours
  D. Tax benefits

__C__ 8. A scale drawing that shows how the overall space in a building will be divided is a
  A. layout.
  B. tenant improvement.
  C. floor plan.
  D. lease.

__C__ 9. Which of the following types of space is *not* typically required for a retail business layout?
  A. Customer space
  B. Selling space
  C. Planning space
  D. Storage space

__B__ 10. Which type of floor plan is used by department stores and other stores with a variety of merchandise to encourage customers to make a complete circuit of the store?
  A. Straight floor plan
  B. Loop floor plan
  C. Angular floor plan
  D. Diagonal floor plan

True or False

On the line next to each of the following statements, write *True* if the statement is true, or write *False* if the statement is not true.

__True__ 11. Residential zoning laws deal with issues such as noise and delivery issues.

__True__ 12. The channel through which a product moves from producer to consumer is called the supply chain.

__False__ 13. The party who owns a property that has been leased is the lessee.

__False__ 14. Wholesale businesses generally use an angular layout.

__True__ 15. Local employment agencies can help entrepreneurs find the right talent for their particular businesses.

__True__ 16. Employee theft accounts for more loss of income in retail businesses than consumer shoplifting.

__False__ 17. Purchasing an existing building for your business is usually more expensive than building a new facility.

__True__ 18. In a retail layout, aisles should be an average of 3 feet wide.

Chapter 7 Site Selection   **49**

Name _____

__True__ 19. A free-flow layout tends to encourage impulse buying.

__False__ 20. In a process-based manufacturing layout, machines and equipment are placed along the route materials move in the assembly process.

Matching

Read the numbered definitions. Then, choose the correct term from the list that follows and write the letter on the line provided next to the definition.

__E__ 21. Statistics about the economy that indicate how it is performing.

__A__ 22. Ideas or opinions about beauty.

__I__ 23. The cost to remodel existing interior space for a new business.

__H__ 24. Employees and machines move around a large product, which remains in a fixed position.

__C__ 25. Any business process conducted using computers or on the Internet.

__J__ 26. Creating floor plans and displays to attract customer attention and encourage purchases.

__F__ 27. Equipment and workers are grouped by division of labor.

__B__ 28. Assigning a worker or group of workers to a specialized task for increased efficiency.

__D__ 29. Buying and selling goods and services through the Internet.

__G__ 30. Machines and equipment are placed along the route materials move through the assembly process.

A. aesthetics
B. division of labor
C. e-business
D. e-commerce
E. economic indicators
F. process-based layout
G. product-based layout
H. project-based layout
I. tenant improvement
J. visual merchandising

Part 2: Activate Your Understanding

Chapter Activities

Read each scenario and study the building outline to determine an appropriate layout. Within each building outline, sketch the layout you would recommend for the business.

1. Campbell's is a locally-owned grocery store that is about to add a second store location. The store carries frozen foods, fresh produce, canned goods, dairy, and dry staples such as flour and sugar. It also has a meat counter and a fish counter. Mr. Campbell has purchased an existing building for the new store. The building is 6,000 feet wide and 3,000 feet deep, for a total of 18,000 square feet. The entrance is in the middle of one of the 6,000-foot sides, as shown below. Sketch a suitable floor plan.   Student floor plans will vary.

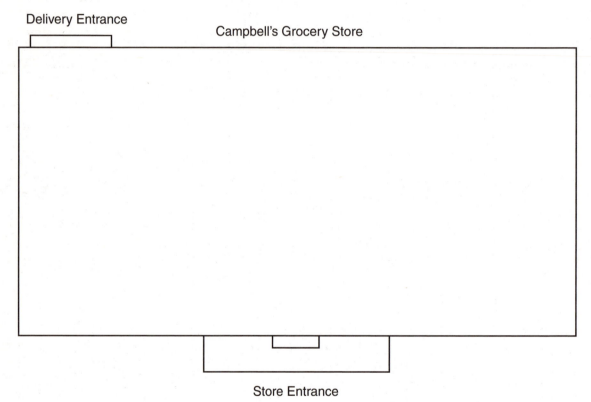

Chapter 7   Site Selection

Name _____

2. Myra is planning to open a small specialty shop called Myra's Fashions. She has found a suitable location in a strip mall located on one of the town's main streets. The store is currently divided into a front room and a back room. The front area is 30 feet wide and 50 feet deep. The back area is 30 feet wide and 20 feet deep, as shown below. Myra does not want to change the position of the interior wall. She plans to sell clothing as well as accessories such as jewelry and scarves. Sketch a suitable floor plan.   Student floor plans will vary.

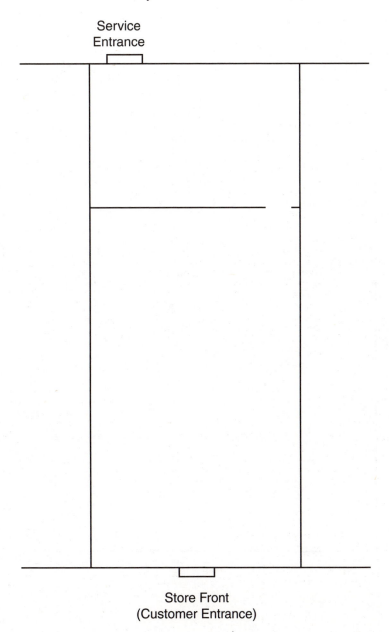

Myra's Fashions

Service Entrance

Store Front
(Customer Entrance)

3. Miguel is preparing to open a new manufacturing company. He plans to manufacture a new electronic device for which he has just received a patent. The device will be assembled on an assembly line as follows:

   A. The electronics will be applied to the main circuit board.

   B. A separate timer will be connected to the main circuit board.

   C. The display LCDs will be put in place.

   D. A power cord will be attached.

   E. A protective case will be added around the inner parts.

   F. The device will be tested at a quality control station.

The building Miguel has purchased has 1,600 square feet and is perfectly square, so each side of the building is 40 feet long. There are two entrances, as shown below. Create a suitable floor plan for Miguel's business.   Student floor plans will vary.

Miguel's Factory

Chapter 7 Site Selection

Name _____

Communication Activities

4. Conduct research to find out more about the zoning laws in your area. How are home businesses treated for zoning purposes? Could you legally start a business in your home? If so, what permits or inspections would you need to obtain? Write an informative report detailing your findings. In the space provided, list the resources you used to gather the information.

   Student answers will vary.

5. Conduct research to find business incentives available in your state. What types of incentives are available, and to what types of businesses? Are any incentives available within your community? In the space provided, list any incentives you find and state the general conditions (location, type of business) to receive the incentive. Give an oral presentation of your findings.

   Student answers will vary.

Math Activities

6. Cecelia is planning to open a shop that features the pottery of local artists. She has already signed up 15 artists, and because the shop is in a tourist town, she anticipates a lot of business. She knows she will not be able to run the store alone. She thinks she can afford to hire up to two people to help her.

   A. What two job positions should Cecelia consider for her employees?

      Student answers will vary. Examples include a sales associate and a bookkeeper, or two sales associates.

   B. Investigate the typical wages for these jobs. If she hires both of the employees you suggested in part A, how much should Cecelia budget for employee salaries?

      Student answers will vary based on the positions students listed in part A.

7. For each of the following scenarios, calculate the sales per square foot.

   A. Carrie's Boutique has total net sales of $935,400 and 12,000 square feet of selling space.

   Sales per square foot: $77.95 per square foot

   B. A department store has total net sales of $12,365,000 and 38,000 square feet of selling space.

   Sales per square foot: $325.39 per square foot

CHAPTER 8: Legal Issues

Part 1: Check Your Knowledge

Multiple Choice

Write the letter of the correct answer to each question on the line provided.

__D__ 1. Which of the following is *not* a type of business law?
   A. Laws to protect personal information from theft
   B. Laws to protect intellectual property
   C. Laws that regulate truth in advertising
   D. Laws that regulate personal health care programs

__B__ 2. The type of law that deals with relationships between an owner and an agent is
   A. common law.
   B. agency law.
   C. criminal law.
   D. property law.

__C__ 3. OSHA is an example of a(n)
   A. compensation-and-benefits law.
   B. equal-employment-opportunity law.
   C. health-and-safety law.
   D. consumer-protection law.

__A__ 4. To protect entrepreneurial ideas, it is important to have
   A. intellectual property laws.
   B. SBA approval.
   C. Federal Trade Commission support.
   D. consumer protection laws.

__B__ 5. Consumer protection laws are those laws that
   A. protect manufacturers from consumer complaints.
   B. protect consumers from unsafe products.
   C. protect products from misuse by consumers.
   D. protect manufacturers from product failure.

__B__ 6. Which of the following marks can be used without being formally registered?
   A. Service mark
   B. Graphic mark
   C. Trademark
   D. Patent

__D__ 7. Which of the following is *not* a patent category?
   A. Design patent
   B. Utility patent
   C. Plant patent
   D. Data patent

__C__ 8. Equal-employment-opportunity laws ensure that all workers are given equal opportunity for
   A. earning the minimum wage.
   B. collective bargaining.
   C. employment in the workplace.
   D. access to health insurance.

__A__ 9. The use of intellectual property without permission is considered
   A. infringement.
   B. breach of contract.
   C. discrimination.
   D. harassment.

__D__ 10. What must businesses with employees obtain from the IRS to track income taxes withheld from employee paychecks?
   A. Business license
   B. Occupational license
   C. Sales tax identification number
   D. Employee identification number

True or False

On the line next to each of the following statements, write *True* if the statement is true, or write *False* if the statement is not true.

__True__ 11. In a business contract, the term *party* refers to a person or group entering into an agreement.

__False__ 12. A tort can be either a civil or a criminal offense.

__False__ 13. A breach of contract is considered a tort.

__True__ 14. A monopoly is a business that has complete control of the supply of goods or services in a market.

__False__ 15. Collective bargaining is a negotiation between employers regarding benefits to offer their employees.

__True__ 16. A person who is denied a job because she is "too old for the job" is experiencing workplace discrimination.

__False__ 17. The purpose of a recall is to punish the company that put a faulty product on the market.

Chapter 8 Legal Issues

Name _____

__False__ 18. In general, seeking legal advice before signing a contract is an unnecessary expense for an entrepreneur.

__True__ 19. Mutual acceptance is *not* valid if the seller pressures the buyer into purchasing a product.

__True__ 20. An original idea is an example of intellectual property.

Matching

Read the numbered definitions. Then, choose the correct term from the list that follows and write the letter on the line provided next to the definition.

__C__ 21. Protects music, writings, paintings, and other original works of authorship.

__A__ 22. Someone who works on a business owner's behalf.

__I__ 23. A fee paid to a professional in advance for services.

__F__ 24. A proposal to provide a service or product.

__D__ 25. Any use of intellectual property without permission.

__G__ 26. Gives a person or company the right to be the sole producer of a product for a defined period of time.

__J__ 27. Protects taglines, slogans, names, symbols, and other methods of identifying a product or company.

__E__ 28. Both parties agree to the terms of an offer.

__H__ 29. Removes an unsafe product from the market.

__B__ 30. Something of value.

A. agent
B. consideration
C. copyright
D. infringement
E. mutual acceptance
F. offer
G. patent
H. recall
I. retainer
J. trademark

Part 2: Activate Your Understanding

Chapter Activities

1. Contracts

    Read each of the following scenarios and decide whether it describes a legally enforceable contract. For each item, record the contract condition that was or was not met.

    A. A 16-year-old TV star signs an agreement with a real estate agent to purchase a $5 million house in Beverly Hills, CA.

    Is this contract legally enforceable? _____

    Condition: No. The party is not yet 18 years old.

B. An eye doctor's office pressures new patients to take a $60 eye exam before making an appointment to see the eye doctor. If a patient accepts this offer of an eye exam, is the contract between the eye doctor's office and the patient legal?

Is this contract legally enforceable? _____

Condition: No. The seller (the eye doctor's office) pressured the potential buyer to take the eye exam, so the contract is not legally executed.

C. A babysitter looked after the neighbor's child for five hours. When the child's parents returned home, they said, "Thank you" to the babysitter and paid $50 as promised. Was there a consideration involved?

Was a consideration involved in this transaction? _____

Condition: Yes. The money and the hours spent babysitting were the considerations.

D. A private collector agreed to purchase a painting that had been stolen from an art gallery and promised, in writing, to pay $1 million in cash.

Is this contract legally enforceable? _____

Condition: No. Contracts involving criminal acts are not enforceable because selling stolen goods is a crime.

E. A car dealer gave his word that a $50,000 luxury sports car would be delivered to the buyer in two weeks. No papers were signed.

Does this constitute a legally binding contract? _____

Condition: No. Verbal contracts are valid only for goods or services that are worth less than $500.

2. Intellectual Property

Fill in the table below to compare and contrast the various forms of protection for intellectual property.

Type of Protection	Type of Intellectual Property Protected	How to Obtain	Length of Protection
Patent	Functional or mechanical inventions	File application with US Patent and Trademark Office	14 to 20 years
Trademark	Unique methods of identifying a company, such as a tagline, slogan, or symbol	Register with the US Patent and Trademark Office	Never expires
Copyright	Original works of authorship, such as music, writings, or paintings	Assigned automatically as soon as the work is in tangible form, but can be registered with the US Copyright Office	Life of the author plus 70 years

Chapter 8 Legal Issues

Name _____

3. Effect of Workplace Laws on Entrepreneurs

The following table lists the four main groups of workplace laws. Think about the direct impact that these laws may have on your business. Complete the table by writing a short summary explaining why each of these laws is important to your business or to entrepreneurs in general.

Type of Workplace Laws	Importance to Entrepreneurs
Labor-Relations Laws	Student answers will vary.
Health-and-Safety Laws	
Compensation-and-Benefits Laws	
Equal-Employment-Opportunity Laws	

Communication Activities

4. Conduct research to find out what kind of insurance offers business owners protection against torts and civil lawsuits. Write an informative report about this form of insurance, including common policy limits and approximate cost to the business owner. In the space provided, record the sources you used to create your report.

   Student answers will vary.

   _____

   _____

5. Conduct research to find out more about the Federal Trade Commission. Prepare an informative report describing the history and purpose of the FTC. In the space provided, list the information you found.

   A. When was the FTC created, and what was its original purpose?

   The FTC was created in 1914 with the original purpose of preventing unfair competition due

   to trusts.

   _____

   B. What are the three current strategic goals of the FTC?

   The three current strategic goals of the FTC are to protect consumers by preventing fraud,

   deception, and unfair business practices; to maintain competition by preventing mergers

   and other practices that would encourage monopoly; and to advance the FTC's own

   performance.

   _____

   _____

6. Conduct research to find a product that has been recalled in the last few months. Find out why the product was recalled, how many of the product were involved, and what people should do if they own the affected product. Prepare an oral presentation about the recall and present it to the class. In the space provided, list the item you researched and the source(s) you used to find this information.

Product recalled: _Student answers will vary._

Source(s): _____

_____

_____

Chapter 9: Business Funding

Part 1: Check Your Knowledge

Multiple Choice

Write the letter of the correct answer to each question on the line provided.

__A__ 1. Cash invested in the business for the purpose of making a profit is called
   A. equity capital.
   B. trade credit.
   C. debt financing.
   D. peer-to-peer lending.

__D__ 2. Bootstrapping involves
   A. operating on as much cash as possible.
   B. using your business finances for personal purposes.
   C. keeping your personal and business assets separately.
   D. cutting all unnecessary expenses.

__C__ 3. The amount of ownership a person has in a business is called
   A. fixed assets.
   B. liquid assets.
   C. equity.
   D. trade credit.

__C__ 4. Equity financing options include all of the following *except*
   A. personal savings.
   B. venture capitalists.
   C. banks and credit unions.
   D. family and friends.

__B__ 5. Exchanging products or services for other products or services, with no money exchanged, is called
   A. bootstrapping.
   B. barter.
   C. venture capital.
   D. equity capital.

__A__ 6. Which of the following statements about a line of credit is *not* true?
  A. It is a loan of unlimited funds for an unlimited time.
  B. It is a loan of a specific amount of money.
  C. It has a specific interest rate.
  D. It must be paid off in regular installments.

__D__ 7. Which of the following is *not* an example of variable expenses?
  A. Utilities
  B. Insurance
  C. Advertising
  D. Salaries

__B__ 8. The financial progress of a business is shown in the pro forma
  A. cash flow statement.
  B. income statement.
  C. balance sheet.
  D. financial statement.

__C__ 9. Which of the following is *not* one of the five Cs of banking?
  A. Cash flow
  B. Collateral
  C. Cosigner
  D. Conditions

__A__ 10. Another term for *owner's equity* is
  A. net worth.
  B. marginal cost.
  C. marginal benefit.
  D. liability.

True or False

On the line next to each of the following statements, write *True* if the statement is true, or write *False* if the statement is not true.

__False__ 11. A business plan must include paying an owner salary from the first month of operation.

__False__ 12. Equity financing is money borrowed from a bank.

__True__ 13. The Small Business Administration does *not* loan money directly to business owners.

__False__ 14. Microloans and 7(a) loans are examples of social lending.

__True__ 15. Debt financing is money that must be repaid with interest.

__False__ 16. Another term for *venture capitalists* is angel investors.

__False__ 17. The *rule of two* states that you should purchase two of every type of equipment so that you have a spare on hand.

__True__ 18. Accurate pricing of products and services is crucial to business success.

__True__ 19. A lender may review an owner's personal financial status along with the financial status of the business.

__False__ 20. The amount by which product sales exceed the cost to the business of producing them is known as the business' operating capital.

Chapter 9   Business Funding

Name _____

Matching

Read the numbered definitions. Then, choose the correct term from the list that follows and write the letter on the line provided next to the definition.

__D__ 21. Borrowing money for business purposes.

__C__ 22. The amount of revenue a business must generate in order to equal its expenses.

__H__ 23. Borrowing money from investors via a website.

__J__ 24. One business granting a line of credit to another business for the purchase of goods and services.

__F__ 25. The money needed to support day-to-day business operations.

__B__ 26. Money owed to a business by customers for goods or services delivered.

__G__ 27. The difference between a company's assets and its liabilities.

__I__ 28. The cash used to start a business.

__A__ 29. Money a business owes to suppliers for goods or services received.

__E__ 30. Raising money for a business in exchange for a percentage of ownership.

A. accounts payable
B. accounts receivable
C. break-even point
D. debt financing
E. equity financing
F. operating capital
G. owner's equity
H. peer-to-peer lending
I. start-up capital
J. trade credit

Part 2: Activate Your Understanding

Chapter Activities

1. Five Cs of Banking

    When you apply for a business loan, the bank will evaluate your loan application using the five Cs of banking. How will you, as a young entrepreneur, satisfy these requirements? Think of examples that may satisfy the banker and write them in the following table.

Five Cs of Banking	Examples of How You Meet (or Plan to Meet) the Requirements
Character	Student answers will vary.
Cash Flow	
Capital	
Collateral	
Conditions	

2. Pro Forma Balance Sheet

   Using the template below, prepare a pro forma balance sheet for your start-up business. Be specific, and be sure to list all of your assets and liabilities items. Use the following information:
   - You saved $1,500 from your job working at the golf course last summer.
   - You received a new laptop computer worth $1,200 as a gift from your parents.
   - You borrowed $800 (no-interest 1-year loan) from your parents to purchase software.
   - You designed flyers for a political campaign, and the customer's payment of $500 is due to you this week.
   - You borrowed your brother's printer, but you paid $70 for ink and paper.
   - You work out of your room at home, so your parents are paying the utilities.

   Name of Your Business: __Business name and date will vary.__

   Pro Forma Balance Sheet

   Date: _____

ASSETS	
Cash	$1,500
Equipment	
1. Laptop computer	$1,200
2. Ink, paper	$70
3.	
Accounts Receivable	$500
Total Assets	$3,270
LIABILITIES	
Accounts Payable	
Notes Payable	$800
Total Liabilities	
OWNER'S EQUITY	
Capital	
Total Liabilities and Owner's Equity	$2,470

Chapter 9   Business Funding

65

Name _____

3. Financing Your Business

   As you start your own business, you need to find sources of cash to finance it. In the space provided, briefly describe your business, and explain what would be the best types of financing for it and why. Will you choose self-funding, equity financing, debt financing, or a combination of these methods?

   Description of your business: _Student answers will vary._

   _____

   _____

   _____

   _____

   Financing: _____

   _____

   _____

   _____

   _____

   _____

   _____

Math Activities

4. Reanna is estimating the start-up costs for her new coffee shop business. After checking supply prices, she estimates that the equipment will cost about $12,000. Stock (coffee, snacks, condiments, paper cups, etc.) will cost about $450 per month. She hasn't chosen a location yet, but suitable buildings in the area lease for an average of $1,500 per month. She checks with other business owners in the area and learns that utilities cost an average of $345 per month. She plans to pay herself a salary of $3,000 per month starting in the ninth month of her first year. Using the rule of two, calculate how much start-up capital Reanna needs. Show your work in the space provided.

Equipment	$12,000
Stock: ($450 × 12 months)	$5,400
Lease ($1,500 × 12 months)	$18,000
Utilities ($345 × 12 months)	$4,140
Salary ($3,000 × 4 months)	$12,000
Total:	$51,540
Start-up capital needed: use rule of two (total estimate × 2) =	$103,080

   Start-up capital needed: _____

5. Jay has created the following sales forecast for his computer repair business. He plans to start the business on January 2, and he knows it will take a while to build up the business. He thinks he has estimated a fair number of hours for each month.

   A. Calculate the total sales for each month and record them in the appropriate place in the sales forecast table.   (See table.)

   B. Jay did not use the *rule of two* when he created his sales forecast. Apply the *rule of two* and estimate Jay's total sales for the year.

   Total sales: __$28,000__

Jay's Computer Repair Sales Forecast for 20--												
	Jan	Feb	Mar	Apr	May	Jun	Jul	Aug	Sep	Oct	Nov	Dec
Hours	15	20	20	30	35	40	40	40	40	40	40	40
Hourly Rate	$35	$35	$35	$35	$35	$35	$35	$35	$35	$35	$35	$35
Total Sales	$525	$700	$700	$1,050	$1,225	$1,400	$1,400	$1,400	$1,400	$1,400	$1,400	$1,400

6. Estimate the start-up costs for your business. If you have not decided on a specific business, choose a type of business you might like to start. Conduct research to determine the start-up costs for a business of this type in your area. Record your answers in the table. If an item does not apply to your business, write "N/A" next to the item. Total the yearly expenses in the last row. Be sure to include the cost for 12 months of each of the monthly expenses.

Your Business: _____	
Brief Description of Your Business:	
Start-Up Item	**Estimated Cost**
Initial Expenses	Student answers will vary.
Furniture	
Equipment	
DBA license	
Business license	
Utility deposits	
Initial inventory	
Other:	
Other:	
Total Initial Expenses	
Monthly Expenses (Ongoing)	
Lease	
Utilities	
Inventory	
Employee wages	
Other:	
Other:	
Other:	
Total Monthly Expenses (per Year)	
Total Expenses for First Year	

Name _____ Date _____ Period _____

CHAPTER 10
Product, Price, and Place

Part 1: Check Your Knowledge

Multiple Choice

Write the letter of the correct answer to each question on the line provided.

__B__ 1. Expenses that do not change and are not affected by the number of products produced or sold are
   A. variable expenses.
   B. fixed expenses.
   C. bonuses.
   D. markup.

__A__ 2. In the marketing mix, the product's life cycle will affect and influence
   A. price.
   B. promotion.
   C. placement.
   D. positioning.

__D__ 3. A picture, design, or image that is associated with a brand is a(n)
   A. association mark.
   B. slogan.
   C. tagline.
   D. logo.

__C__ 4. The percentage of the total sales of a specific product that one company conducts is the company's
   A. product cycle.
   B. return on investment.
   C. market share.
   D. price incentive.

__A__ 5. The point at which a company's sales equal expenses is the company's
   A. break-even point.
   B. market share.
   C. return on investment.
   D. product life cycle.

Copyright Goodheart-Willcox Co., Inc.

__D__ 6. A working model of a new product that is made for testing purposes is a(n)
   A. intermediary.
   B. tagline.
   C. brand.
   D. prototype.

__D__ 7. The pricing method that focuses on what customers are willing to pay is called
   A. cost-based pricing.
   B. keystone pricing.
   C. psychological pricing.
   D. demand-based pricing.

__B__ 8. Determining a product's selling price by doubling the total cost of the product is
   A. demand-based pricing.
   B. keystone pricing.
   C. competition-based pricing.
   D. psychological pricing.

__C__ 9. The price of a product that is printed in a catalog or on the price tag and does *not* include any discounts is the
   A. selling price.
   B. MSRP.
   C. list price.
   D. keystone price.

__A__ 10. A group of closely related products within a product mix are called a product
   A. line.
   B. width.
   C. depth.
   D. item.

True or False

On the line next to each of the following statements, write *True* if the statement is true, or write *False* if the statement is not true.

__True__ 11. A company's variable expenses change based on the activity of the business.

__False__ 12. The price the customer pays for a product after discounts or coupons are applied is the MSRP.

__True__ 13. Psychological pricing is a technique that is used to make prices seem attractive to customers.

__True__ 14. A retailer is an example of an intermediary.

__False__ 15. A trade discount is a special price that encourages customers to buy at off-peak times of the year.

__True__ 16. A broker's job is to bring a buyer and a seller together.

__False__ 17. The satisfaction a customer receives from owning a product is known as place utility.

__False__ 18. Product depth is the number of product lines a company offers.

Chapter 10   Product, Price, and Place

Name _____

__False__ 19. Setting very low prices to drive competitors out of business is a pricing practice called price-fixing.

__True__ 20. When the demand for a product is low and supply is high, the price of the product may be lowered to encourage people to buy it.

Matching

Read the numbered definitions. Then, choose the correct term from the list that follows and write the letter on the line provided next to the definition.

__G__ 21. A measure of profitability that is based on the amount earned from investment in a business.

__B__ 22. The desired amount of profit added to a product's cost.

__J__ 23. The relative worth of something to a person.

__A__ 24. The path that goods take through the supply chain.

__E__ 25. All of the goods and services that a business sells.

__H__ 26. A measure of profitability that is equal to the company's net income divided by total sales.

__C__ 27. The stages a product goes through from the beginning to the end.

__I__ 28. Coordinating the events that happen throughout the supply chain.

__D__ 29. A group of closely related products within a company's product mix.

__F__ 30. Distinguishing the company's products from competing products.

A. channel of distribution
B. markup
C. product life cycle
D. product line
E. product mix
F. product positioning
G. return on investment
H. return on sales
I. supply chain management
J. value

Part 2: Activate Your Understanding

Chapter Activities

1. Pricing a Product

   Sometimes the price of a particular brand of a product may seem out of line with the prices of similar products. Lip balm is a good example. Conduct research to find out more about each of the following products: ChapStick®, Carmex®, and Kisstixx®. Review the price and the description or advertising for each product, and record this information in the table. In the space provided below the table, explain why one product is priced so much higher than the other two.

Product	Price	Description or Advertising
ChapStick®		Student answers will vary, but students should find that Kisstixx® costs roughly three times as much as the other two products. Rationales will vary, but students should realize that this is an example of prestige pricing.
Carmex®		
Kisstixx®		

2. Packaging a Product

   Sometimes, products we use every day may be packaged differently to give the product a fresh new look or to appeal to a different market. For example, chewing gum used to be packaged in long, flat sticks until Orbit® and other brands introduced shorter, thicker offerings. Choose a product you use often, such as a pair of shoes or a smartphone. Research various types of packaging techniques that could be applied to the product. Design a new type of packaging for the product. Create a drawing of the packaging. If resources are available, you may want to create a prototype also. In the space provided, explain why your packaging is an improvement on the product's current packaging.

   Student answers will vary.

Chapter 10 Product, Price, and Place

Name _____

3. New Product Development

With a partner, work through the stages of product development listed in the table. Record your ideas and decisions in the table. For step 4, determine the cost to produce your product and determine how much you would charge for the product. For step 6, build a prototype if possible, but if the resources are not available, list the materials that would be needed to build the prototype.

Stage in New Product Development	Ideas, Decisions, and Plans
1. Idea generation	Student answers will vary.
2. Conduct research	
3. Investigate a concept	
4. Analyze the finances	
5. Design the product	
6. Build a prototype	
7. Market the product	

4. Product Life Cycle

Locate examples of products in each of the four stages of the product life cycle. Complete the table below to identify the products and provide a rationale stating why you believe the products are in these stages.

Stage of Product Life Cycle	Product Name	Rationale
Introduction	Student answers will vary.	
Growth		
Maturity		
Decline		

Math Activities

5. Calculate the return on sales for each of the following companies. Round your answers to the nearest tenth of a percent.

   A. A jewelry store has a net income of $43,500 and total sales of $94,200.

   Return on sales: _____ $43,500 ÷ $94,200 = 0.461783 or 46.2% _____

   B. A specialty shop has a net income of $56,100 and total sales of $82,400.

   Return on sales: _____ $56,100 ÷ $82,400 = 0.680825 or 68.1% _____

   C. A department store has a net income of $176,000 and total sales of $421,700.

   Return on sales: _____ $176,000 ÷ $421,700 = 0.417358 or 41.7% _____

6. Calculate the return on investment for each of the following companies. Round your answers to the nearest tenth of a percent.

   A. An electronics store has total assets of $356,000 and a net profit of $65,400.

   Return on investment: _____ $65,400 ÷ $356,000 = 0.183708 or 18.4% _____

   B. An auto parts store has total assets of $226,000 and a net profit of $52,700.

   Return on investment: _____ $52,700 ÷ $226,000 = 0.233186 or 23.3% _____

   C. A furniture store has total assets of $589,200 and a net profit of $246,100.

   Return on investment: _____ $246,100 ÷ $589,200 = 0.417685 or 41.8% _____

7. A telecommunications company sells a certain brand of smartphone for $199. The company has purchased 150 of the smartphones for $125 each. Perform a break-even analysis. How many smartphones must be sold to reach the break-even point for this product? Round your answer to the next highest whole number.

   ($125 × 150) ÷ $199 = $18,750 ÷ $199 = 94.22 or 95 smartphones

Name _____ Date _____ Period _____

CHAPTER 11: Promotion and Selling

Part 1: Check Your Knowledge

Multiple Choice

Write the letter of the correct answer to each question on the line provided.

__C__ 1. The type of communication used to motivate people to buy a product or service is known as
   A. packaging.
   B. launching.
   C. promotion.
   D. public relations.

__B__ 2. A form of communication that is paid for by sponsors to help persuade consumers to buy a product or service is
   A. circulation.
   B. advertising.
   C. personal selling.
   D. public relations.

__D__ 3. Activities that promote goodwill between a business and the public are called
   A. push promotions.
   B. pull promotions.
   C. advertising.
   D. public relations.

__A__ 4. Software programs that allow people to access promotions and product information using mobile devices such as smartphones and tablets are commonly known as
   A. mobile apps.
   B. text messaging.
   C. push promotions.
   D. pull promotions.

__A__ 5. An Internet-based tool that connects people with similar interests and allows companies to share information with their customers is
   A. social media.
   B. public relations.
   C. broadcast media.
   D. advertising.

__B__ 6. The process of indexing a website so that it ranks higher on the list when people search the Internet is called
   A. digital presence search.
   B. search engine optimization.
   C. e-mail campaigning.
   D. web-design indexing.

__A__ 7. A bar code that allows consumers to go directly to a company's website is a(n)
   A. QR code.
   B. URL.
   C. wiki link.
   D. SEO.

__C__ 8. When a campaign promotes the company itself, rather than a particular product or service, the company is using
   A. public relations.
   B. placement.
   C. institutional promotion.
   D. advertising.

__B__ 9. Placing ads on websites whose typical viewers are the target market for a company's products is known as
   A. traditional advertising.
   B. web advertising.
   C. e-mail campaigns.
   D. personal selling.

__D__ 10. The digital strategy in which customers actively seek out the product using mobile apps or QR codes is the
   A. push promotional strategy.
   B. institutional promotional strategy.
   C. social promotional strategy.
   D. pull promotional strategy.

True or False

On the line next to each of the following statements, write *True* if the statement is true, or write *False* if the statement is not true.

__False__ 11. Pop-up ads are most prevalent in traditional advertising media, such as newspapers.

__True__ 12. The four Ps of marketing are price, promotion, place, and product.

__True__ 13. Twitter, Facebook, and YouTube are examples of social media.

__False__ 14. Persuading customers to buy a product or service is known as coercion.

__True__ 15. Tracking the number of website hits after a promotion goes live is an example of metrics.

__True__ 16. Advertising to create demand for a product before the product is available is known as preselling.

__False__ 17. Transit promotion is a type of broadcast media.

__False__ 18. Infomercials are a form of public relations.

Chapter 11 Promotion and Selling

Name _____

__False__ 19. A native app is a mobile software application that resides on the website, rather than the mobile device.

__True__ 20. The process of finding potential customers is known as prospecting.

Matching

Read the numbered definitions. Then, choose the correct term from the list that follows and write the letter on the line provided next to the definition.

__I__ 21. An organized method or approach to product sales.

__G__ 22. Unpaid media coverage for a newsworthy business, person, or product.

__C__ 23. Ways to measure the effectiveness of a promotion.

__A__ 24. A buying process model that includes attention, interest, desire, and action.

__D__ 25. Any direct contact between a salesperson and a customer.

__J__ 26. The unique address of a document, web page, or website on the Internet.

__E__ 27. A meeting with media representatives that is arranged by a business or organization.

__B__ 28. The number of copies of printed ads distributed to subscribers and other outlets.

__F__ 29. A packet of information about a business that is distributed to the media.

__H__ 30. Expected sales for a specific time period.

A. AIDA
B. circulation
C. metrics
D. personal selling
E. press conference
F. press kit
G. publicity
H. sales quota
I. selling process
J. uniform resource locator

Part 2: Activate Your Understanding

Chapter Activities

1. Institutional Promotion

    Work with a partner to come up with a new business idea. Determine the best way to promote your new business. Remember, this is not a product promotion, but rather promotion of the business itself. Consider both traditional and digital promotional strategies. Create a promotional plan for the business that includes at least three different strategies. List your strategies in the space provided.

    Strategy A: __Student strategies will vary.__

    _____

    _____

    _____

Strategy B: _____

_____

_____

_____

Strategy C: _____

_____

_____

_____

2. Product Promotion

    Obtain an existing product of your choice. Devise a promotional strategy to promote this product to the class. Create promotional material using print media to assist in your promotional presentation. Describe your promotional strategy in the space provided.

    Student strategies will vary.
    _____
    _____
    _____
    _____
    _____

3. Create an advertising campaign for a product with which you are familiar. First, choose the product. Then identify the target market. Finally, suggest an advertising campaign that you believe will make people in the target market want to buy the product. Record your ideas in the space provided.

    Product name: _____

    Target market: _____

    _____

    Ideas for advertising campaign: _____

    Student answers will vary, but their ideas should reflect the target market for the product they have chosen.
    _____
    _____
    _____
    _____

Chapter 11 Promotion and Selling

Name _____

4. Radio advertisements are fairly inexpensive and provide easy access to hundreds of listeners. Radio ads pose specific challenges, however. There is no visual—the potential customers cannot see the product you are advertising. Also, radio ads must be very brief. Most radio stations sell ad "spots" of 15, 30, and 60 seconds.

   For this activity, develop a 15-second advertisement for a new hair styling salon. Pay careful attention to timing. Try to capture the interest of radio listeners and convince them to try the new salon. If equipment is available, record your ad and play it for the class. If no equipment is available, read your advertisement to the class. Have someone time the ad to make sure it falls within the 15 seconds allowed. In the space provided, list the main points you will cover in your radio advertisement.

   Student answers will vary.

5. Develop a plan for a contest or sweepstakes to promote a new type of bicycle helmet. Consider the target market and make the prizes something the potential customers will want. In the space provided, describe your plans for the contest or sweepstakes and explain how this promotion will help capture data for the company that sells the bicycle helmets.

   Student answers will vary.

6. Visit four different Internet sites that display banner ads or other forms of advertising. Analyze the effectiveness of the ads and their relevance to the target market. Complete the table to record your findings. In the space below, name the ad you found most effective, and explain why.

Internet Site (Site name and URL)	Effectiveness	Relevance to Target Market
1.		
2.		
3.		
4.		

Most effective ad: _Student answers will vary._

Why? _____

_____

_____

_____

7. Create a press release for an event to support a local or national charity, such as the American Cancer Society or the American Red Cross. Conduct research to find out more about the charity you have chosen and the types of events the charity holds. Be sure to avoid using an article or advertisement format. You may want to conduct research to find a suitable format to use. Record the content of your press release in the space provided.

Student answers will vary.

Name _____ Date _____ Period _____

Marketing Plan

Part 1: Check Your Knowledge

Multiple Choice

Write the letter of the correct answer to each question on the line provided.

__D__ 1. The purpose of marketing is to
   A. find financial backers.
   B. analyze the competition.
   C. discover new product ideas.
   D. generate customer transactions.

__B__ 2. The document that defines a company's marketing objectives and the strategies and tactics to achieve them is the
   A. place strategy.
   B. marketing plan.
   C. situation analysis.
   D. action plan.

__A__ 3. In addition to being specific, measurable, attainable, and realistic, marketing plan goals should be
   A. time-based.
   B. thought-provoking.
   C. temporary.
   D. team-oriented.

__B__ 4. Decisions about the marketing mix include decisions about the product, the price of the product, promotions for the product, and
   A. sales force needed to sell the product.
   B. how and where to sell the product.
   C. the life cycle of the product.
   D. how to meet government regulations.

__C__ 5. One indication of the effectiveness of a marketing campaign is
   A. forecasting.
   B. customer satisfaction.
   C. return on investment.
   D. situation analysis.

Copyright Goodheart-Willcox Co., Inc.   79

__A__ 6. Decisions about advertising and public-relations activities are considered
   A. promotion strategies.
   B. place strategies.
   C. price strategies.
   D. product strategies.

__D__ 7. A detailed schedule of tactical activities for a marketing plan is known as a(n)
   A. tracking spreadsheet.
   B. product forecast.
   C. budget.
   D. action plan.

__A__ 8. The specific activities used to carry out marketing strategies are called
   A. marketing tactics.
   B. institutional promotion.
   C. price strategies.
   D. action plans.

__C__ 9. Which of the following is *not* a good source for marketing plan templates?
   A. Universities
   B. Chambers of commerce
   C. Competition
   D. Small Business Administration

__B__ 10. Which of the following is *not* included in a marketing plan?
   A. Marketing tactics
   B. Financial analysis
   C. Action plan
   D. Situation analysis

True or False

On the line next to each of the following statements, write *True* if the statement is true, or write *False* if the statement is not true.

__True__ 11. The target market is defined in the marketing plan for a product.

__True__ 12. A marketing plan details the four Ps of the marketing mix.

__False__ 13. SMART goals do not have to be time-based.

__False__ 14. *Promotion strategies* include decisions about the cost differences of a product.

__True__ 15. An action plan includes a detailed schedule of tactical activities.

__False__ 16. The four Ps of the marketing mix are product, price, pressure, and promotion.

__True__ 17. Pricing policies affect a company's image.

__True__ 18. The style of a company's marketing plan should be similar to the style of its business plan.

__True__ 19. The goals a company wants to achieve during a given time by implementing a marketing plan are known as marketing objectives.

__False__ 20. The purpose of a time line is to keep the company within budget.

Chapter 12 Marketing Plan

Name _____

Matching

Read the numbered definitions. Then, choose the correct term from the list that follows and write the letter on the line provided next to the definition.

__H__ 21. Decisions about quantities to be produced, sizes, packaging, and product design.

__C__ 22. Written document describing a company's marketing objectives and how to meet them.

__F__ 23. Decisions about where to sell products and how to distribute them.

__B__ 24. Goals a business wants to achieve in a given time by implementing a marketing plan.

__I__ 25. Decisions about advertising, electronic promotions, sales promotions, and public-relations activities.

__A__ 26. A plan that sorts out all the details of the marketing tactics for a product.

__J__ 27. A snapshot of the environment in which a business is operating at a given time.

__E__ 28. The specific activities to carry out marketing strategies.

__G__ 29. Decisions about the markup, profit margin, discounts, and list price versus selling price.

__D__ 30. Decisions made about product, price, place, and promotion.

A. action plan
B. marketing objective
C. marketing plan
D. marketing strategies
E. marketing tactics
F. place strategies
G. price strategies
H. product strategies
I. promotion strategies
J. situation analysis

Part 2: Activate Your Understanding

Chapter Activities

1. SMART Goals

   Analyze each of the following goals. List the SMART goal elements that are missing from each goal. Then rewrite each goal to satisfy the requirements of SMART goals.

   A. Within the next 12 months, we will increase product sales by hiring more sales staff.

   Missing elements:
   This goal is relevant, time-based, and presumably attainable, but it is not specific or measurable.

   Rewritten goal:
   Student answers will vary. Example: Within the next 12 months, we will increase product sales by 25% by hiring and training three new salespeople.

B. We will decrease customer complaints by 100% by requiring all customer service representatives to attend hands-on workshops on meeting customer needs.

<u>This goal is specific and probably measurable, but it is not time-based, and it is probably not attainable. Decreasing customer complaints by 100% would mean no customers would complain. This is the ideal, but it is rarely achieved.</u>

Rewritten goal:

<u>Student answers will vary. Example: Within the next six months, we will decrease customer complaints by 80% by requiring all customer service representatives to attend hands-on workshops on meeting customer needs.</u>

2. Marketing Mix

A company is developing a new type of battery-operated cell phone/smartphone charger that is suitable for use on hiking and camping trips. The charger is waterproof and is designed to withstand both heat and humidity. Use the four Ps of marketing to determine the marketing mix for this new product. Use your imagination and creativity to fill in the table below, but make sure your suggestions are reasonable.

Product Strategies	
Quantity to manufacture	Student answers will vary.
Size	
Packaging	
Warranty	
Brand name	
Design (include small sketch)	
Benefits	
Price Strategies	
Markup	
Profit margin	
Discounts, if any	
List price/selling price	
Place Strategies	
Where and how will products be sold?	
What distribution channels will be used?	
Is warehousing necessary? If so, describe.	
Promotion Strategies	
Advertising plans	
Electronic promotions	
Sales promotions	
Public relations	
Who will handle each?	

Chapter 12   Marketing Plan

Name _____

3. Conduct research to obtain two different (free) marketing plan templates. Compare and contrast the templates.

   A. How are the templates similar?

   Student answers will vary, but all marketing templates have the same basic parts.

   B. How are the templates different from one another?

   Student answers will vary. Differences may be based on the type of business to which the marketing plan is geared or the type of product or service being marketed.

4. A company that sells all-natural products has developed a cream that cools sunburn and helps prevent skin peeling. One of the company's marketing tactics is to offer "buy one, get one free" coupons to beachgoers. Create an action plan to describe how this tactic can be implemented efficiently. Record your action plan in the space provided.

   Student answers will vary.

5. Choose a small business in your area. Imagine that you are the owner of the business. Create a brief situation analysis for the business. If you do not have access to some of the information you need, base your responses on your own observations. Record the information in the table.

Situation Analysis	
Name of Business: _____	
Effect of current economic situation on marketing and sales	Student answers will vary.
Target Market	
Competition	

Name _____ Date _____ Period _____

Chapter 13: Management Functions

Part 1: Check Your Knowledge

Multiple Choice

Write the letter of the correct answer to each question on the line provided.

__B__ 1. An individual who is responsible for carrying out the goals of the business is a(n)
   A. mentor.
   B. manager.
   C. accountant.
   D. bookkeeper.

__B__ 2. Which of the following actions is *not* characteristic of an effective manager?
   A. Motivating employees
   B. Micromanaging employees
   C. Delegating work
   D. Treating employees equally

__D__ 3. Someone who guides and directs a person to learn what is needed for a situation is a(n)
   A. entrepreneur.
   B. employee.
   C. leader.
   D. mentor.

__C__ 4. Management is the process of
   A. teaching employees to operate the business by your standards.
   B. explaining to employees how to run the business without your input.
   C. controlling and making decisions about a business.
   D. reaching business goals without regard for efficiency.

__C__ 5. The planning process for a business involves what three specific areas?
   A. Long-term, short-term, and contingency planning
   B. Strategic, tactical, and organizational planning
   C. Tactical, operational, and strategic planning
   D. Staffing, organizational, and tactical planning

__D__ 6. Which of the following is *not* a commonly recognized management style?
   A. Autocratic
   B. Democratic
   C. Laissez-faire
   D. Micromanagement

__A__ 7. The staffing function of management is the process of
   A. hiring the right people for the right jobs.
   B. motivating, directing, and influencing people.
   C. leading, mentoring, and controlling people.
   D. monitoring the performance of employees.

__B__ 8. A manager who allows employees to make their own decisions about how to complete tasks is following which management style?
   A. Consulting style
   B. Laissez-faire style
   C. Autocratic style
   D. Democratic style

__C__ 9. Interpersonal skills are the skills needed to
   A. use time wisely by setting priorities.
   B. solve problems with workflow.
   C. communicate with other people.
   D. visualize the business as a whole.

__A__ 10. An organization's structure of decision-making responsibilities is its
   A. chain of command.
   B. organizational chart.
   C. business plan.
   D. operational plan.

True or False

On the line next to each of the following statements, write *True* if the statement is true, or write *False* if the statement is not true.

__True__ 11. Operational planning determines the day-to-day goals for the company.

__False__ 12. An effective manager does *not* take time to understand what motivates people.

__True__ 13. A manager's business skills include job-specific skills needed to perform in a specialized field.

__False__ 14. A democratic manager combines elements of the consultative and autocratic management styles.

__False__ 15. The controlling function of management includes dictating orders to the staff.

__True__ 16. An effective manager is a good communicator who shares information with the rest of the team.

__False__ 17. People are born with leadership skills; these skills cannot be learned.

__False__ 18. The ability to lead by example and model expected behavior is an example of a skill.

Chapter 13 Management Functions

Name _____

__True_____ 19. The democratic management style is also known as the participatory style.

__False_____ 20. Efficient managers do *not* need to delegate tasks.

Matching

Read the numbered definitions. Then, choose the correct term from the list that follows and write the letter on the line provided next to the definition.

__D__ 21. Setting the day-to-day goals for a company.

__B__ 22. Give employees the authority to make decisions.

__I__ 23. Two or more people working together toward the same goal.

__C__ 24. Employees are welcome to talk with a manager at any time.

__G__ 25. Setting the long-term goals for a company.

__F__ 26. Hiring people and matching them to the best position for their talents.

__A__ 27. Monitoring the progress a business has made in meeting its goals and making needed corrections.

__E__ 28. Managing behavior that differs according to the individual circumstances.

__J__ 29. The ability to set priorities and use time wisely.

__H__ 30. Setting the short-term goals for a company.

A. controlling
B. empower
C. open-door policy
D. operational planning
E. situational management
F. staffing
G. strategic planning
H. tactical planning
I. team
J. time-management skills

Part 2: Activate Your Understanding

Chapter Activities

1. Management Styles

   Read the following statements and decide if they describe you as a democratic, autocratic, consulting, or laissez-faire manager. Write the management style in the space provided.

   A. At the daily operational meetings, you listen to the reports of team leaders, encourage the input of colleagues, ask for employee opinions, and then make your final decision.

      Your management style is: ___Consulting_____

   B. As an entrepreneur and a manager of the company you created, you feel that it is your responsibility to dictate orders to the staff and make all of the decisions. You believe that a good manager controls everything, makes decisions quickly, and does not solicit any other opinions.

      Your management style is: ___Autocratic_____

C. You are a CEO of a successful start-up company. Most of your employees are very involved in the business, which keeps them motivated and gives them a sense of belonging. You feel comfortable delegating authority to the staff, giving them responsibility to make the necessary decisions and carry out the job in the way they choose to complete the work.

Your management style is: **Democratic**

D. As a manager, you believe that little involvement from the manager is best. You limit your involvement to setting the tasks for employees and giving them the opportunity to complete these tasks on their own, as the employees see fit.

Your management style is: **Laissez-faire**

2. Business Planning

Tania is in the process of opening a deli in a local mall. She will offer sandwiches, soups, and desserts in a café-like atmosphere. Help Tania get started by proposing business plans for her new business.

Strategic plan: *Student answers will vary, but should contain long-term goals for the new company. Example: Within three years, become an established business with enough customers to consider expanding the café.*

Tactical plan: *Student answers will vary, but should contain short-term goals for the company. Example: Within the next 12 months, begin operating at a profit that allows Tania to draw a regular salary.*

Operational plan: *Student answers will vary, but should contain day-to-day goals for operating the company. Example: By the end of the first month, have an established business base of 120 customers per week.*

Chapter 13   Management Functions

Name _____

3. Staffing

Elias is expanding his "mom-and-pop" grocery store to add a meat counter, a fresh seafood counter, and a larger produce section. He needs to hire people to work at both counters, as well as someone knowledgeable about produce to manage the new produce section. He also wants to hire two additional people to stock the shelves. Read the descriptions of the people who answered his help-wanted ads. Determine which job might be the best fit for each position described above.

A. Janine is just out of high school. She has no work experience, but she is enthusiastic and doesn't mind starting "at the bottom" with a chance to work her way up into a better job. For which job might Elias hire Janine?

Student answers will vary, but since she has no work experience, it might be best to start

her as a stock person.

B. Tim is in his first year of college and is looking for part-time work to help pay his school expenses. He was raised on a farm and often helped out at his family's produce stand in the summers. He likes people and enjoys discussing different food preparation methods.

Student answers will vary, but Tim might be a good fit for the produce department. Whether

he is management material is debatable, and he only wants to work part-time. Elias could try

him in the produce department, or split his duties between stocking and produce until Tim

proves that he can handle the produce department or gains more experience.

C. Georg currently manages the produce department at a large superstore and has an excellent work record. He prefers working at a meat counter, and has applied for that position. He has prior experience working at both a meat counter and a seafood counter.

Student answers will vary. Georg is obviously a good candidate for produce manager, but

he wants to work at the meat counter and has the necessary experience to do so. Elias

might consider hiring Georg to work mostly at the meat counter, but also mentor Tim in the

produce department.

D. Myra's father owned a butcher shop when she was young, and Myra often helped out in the store. She knows the various cuts of meat and is good with customers. She has also worked in a seafood restaurant and knows a lot about how to prepare various seafood dishes. She would like to work at either the meat counter or the seafood counter.

Student answers will vary, but Myra would be useful at either the meat counter or the

seafood counter. Since Elias has another strong candidate for the meat counter, he might

start Myra at the seafood counter and see how both she and Georg work out.

Communication Activities

4. Identify a business that you would like to start as an entrepreneur. In the space provided, draw an organizational chart of your company. Show the levels of management and who reports to whom. Then write a short report (two to three paragraphs) describing the chain of command in your organization.

   Type of business: _____

   Organizational chart:

   Student answers will vary.

5. Choose a successful entrepreneur in the United States. Conduct research to find out more about this person's leadership style. Be careful to use only credible sources. Consider the traits and skills described in this textbook chapter, and compare them with the traits and skills demonstrated by the entrepreneur. Write an informative report describing the characteristics of this entrepreneur and how he or she used them to succeed in the business. Record your sources in the space provided.

   Student answers will vary.

Chapter 13   Management Functions

Name _____

6. You are about to open a new sporting goods store. You don't want a franchise; this will be a local, neighborhood-type store offering sports equipment and accessories. You believe strongly in teamwork and want to include people on your team to contribute to every aspect of your business. In the space provided, list the people and businesses you will include on your team. Then write a short report explaining why and how these people can contribute to the success of your business.

Student answers will vary.
_____
_____
_____
_____
_____

CHAPTER 14: Human Resources Management

Part 1: Check Your Knowledge

Multiple Choice

Write the letter of the correct answer to each question on the line provided.

__C__ 1. The acronym HR stands for
   A. human research.
   B. hiring resources.
   C. human resources.
   D. hiring records.

__B__ 2. Which of the following is *not* a factor to be considered when an entrepreneur decides whether to hire employees?
   A. You have too much work to complete by yourself.
   B. Your high school friend is broke and needs a job.
   C. You can afford to hire employees.
   D. You are prepared to manage and train employees.

__C__ 3. Which of the following is *not* a typical task of a human resources employee?
   A. Managing employee benefits
   B. Training new employees
   C. Accounting and auditing
   D. Complying with employment laws

__A__ 4. To hire employees that best meet a company's needs, the company performs a
   A. job analysis.
   B. job posting.
   C. performance appraisal.
   D. growth projection.

__D__ 5. Staffing is the process of
   A. managing the employees in the organization.
   B. evaluating the need for company reorganization.
   C. compensating employees for their work.
   D. hiring employees that meet the company's needs.

__C__ 6. All of the following are valid methods of evaluating employees, *except*
   A. objective performance appraisal.
   B. subjective performance appraisal.
   C. random performance appraisal.
   D. self-appraisal.

__B__ 7. Which of the following is *not* commonly included in the training of new employees?
   A. Company mission and operations
   B. Current value of the company's stock
   C. Job procedures and performance expectations
   D. Company rules and regulations

__A__ 8. One way to motivate employees is to
   A. provide opportunities for advancement and pay increases.
   B. promote the idea that money is less important than job satisfaction.
   C. explain that performance is important, but job satisfaction is a myth.
   D. notify employees that they are not expected to share creative ideas.

__D__ 9. Which of the following is part of a formal job description but is *not* necessarily part of the job analysis?
   A. Tasks and duties of the position
   B. Skills needed for the position
   C. Education and experience required
   D. Salary range or ranking

__B__ 10. A percentage of a sale that is paid to the salesperson who makes the sale is a
   A. stock option.
   B. commission.
   C. salary.
   D. bonus.

True or False

On the line next to each of the following statements, write *True* if the statement is true, or write *False* if the statement is not true.

__False__ 11. Small businesses are *not* expected to provide their employees with opportunities to grow in the company.

__False__ 12. Nothing motivates employees more than money.

__True__ 13. Providing feedback is an important part of the performance appraisal process.

__False__ 14. As an entrepreneur, you do *not* need to worry about human resources management issues.

__True__ 15. The first step in conflict resolution is to listen.

__False__ 16. Profit sharing is compensation intended to help employees while they look for another job.

__True__ 17. Subjective performance appraisals are based on an employee's behaviors.

__True__ 18. Training in the skills that contribute to an employee's personal growth and career advancement is known as professional development.

Chapter 14 Human Resources Management

Name _____

__True___ 19. The three types of employment tests are ability, performance, and personality tests.

__False__ 20. Most job seekers today use employment agencies to find a job.

Matching

Read the numbered definitions. Then, choose the correct term from the list that follows and write the letter on the line provided next to the definition.

__A__ 21. Extras over and above regular pay that is given to employees by employers.

__F__ 22. Behavior of employer and employees toward each other, especially during contract negotiations.

__B__ 23. Cash reward given to employees who reach certain performance goals.

__E__ 24. A document that provides day-to-day policy information that employees need to know.

__J__ 25. Shares of company stock that employees can purchase at a discount.

__I__ 26. Distribution of the profits to employees, usually on an annual basis.

__C__ 27. A percentage of a sale paid to the salesperson.

__H__ 28. A document that outlines company policies and procedures.

__D__ 29. Wages, salaries, incentives, and benefits.

__G__ 30. One and one-half times an employee's hourly rate.

A. benefits
B. bonus
C. commission
D. compensation
E. employee handbook
F. labor relations
G. overtime pay
H. policy manual
I. profit sharing
J. stock option

Part 2: Activate Your Understanding

Chapter Activities

1. Employee Evaluation

   Read the following description of Elizabeth's job performance. Elizabeth's first performance appraisal is coming up next month. Ms. Watson, the office supervisor, is working on the dental office employees' appraisal forms. Help Ms. Watson by filling out the performance appraisal using the form provided.

   > Elizabeth is a receptionist at Dr. Ginsberg's dental office. She was hired about a year ago, shortly after graduation from high school. Patients admire her radiant personality, and they often comment on her great customer service skills. Elizabeth is a good listener; she is the kind of employee who can be described as a "people" person. She is patient and flexible in rescheduling clients' appointments when necessary. She is professional and effective in communicating with her colleagues in the office and in interactions with insurance companies. Elizabeth is exceptionally proficient with technology. In fact, that was one of the deciding factors in hiring Elizabeth, as Dr. Ginsberg expected her to create electronic files for their patients and eliminate as much paperwork as possible. Elizabeth proved to be quite successful. Not only is her "electronic files" project near completion, but she also programmed the online scheduling of appointments. In addition, Elizabeth volunteered to set up and maintain Dr. Ginsberg's calendar.
   >
   > However, Ms. Watson is very nervous each time Elizabeth is late to work or calls in sick. Ms. Watson and two other older receptionists do not feel very comfortable with computers, and they wish Elizabeth could spend more time training them instead of surfing the Web and communicating with her Facebook friends online during office hours.

   Student answers will vary, but students should realize that although Elizabeth has some outstanding characteristics and abilities, her habit of communicating with friends and surfing the Web does not constitute professional behavior.

Chapter 14   Human Resources Management

Name _____

Performance Appraisal

Employee Name _____   Date _____

Employee Position/Title _____   Supervisor _____

Education (check the highest level achieved)

☐ High School   ☐ Some College   ☐ AA Degree   ☐ BS Degree   ☐ Master/Ph.D.

Instructions for Supervisors:
Rate each characteristic, skill, or qualification from 1 to 4, with "4" being the highest rating and "1" being the lowest. Provide additional comments, if necessary. Calculate the total score and determine the overall rating for the job.

	1	2	3	4	Comments
Personal Characteristics					
Personal appearance, manners					
Cooperation with coworkers					
Reliability and work ethic					
Time management/effectiveness					
Job-Related Characteristics					
Knowledge of the job					
Interpersonal skills					
Productivity					
Customer service skills					
Technology skills					
Other Qualifications and Skills					
Keyboarding and PC skills					
Programming and IT literacy					
Communication skills					
Filing and record management					
Scheduling, answering phones					
Performing office duties					
Total score*:					

* The maximum total score on this form cannot exceed 60 points (15 categories x 4 points), and the minimum total score cannot be less than 15 points (15 categories x 1 point).

Overall rating for the job:

_____ Superior   _____ Above Average   _____ Average   _____ Marginal

Provide an overall job rating based on the following scale:
46–60 points   Superior (exceptional performance, employee may be recommended for promotion)
30–45 points   Above Average (employee is well qualified)
21–29 points   Average (employee is qualified, but some improvements are recommended)
15–20 points   Marginal (employee is barely qualified; specific training and development plan is recommended)

Copyright Goodheart-Willcox Co., Inc.

2. Staffing

Freddy Garcia, the owner of a small start-up company, is pleased to notice that his sales started picking up significantly in the last few months. He realizes that he needs more help to run the daily operations. While he is trying to identify his staffing needs, one thing becomes clear: someone must relieve him from everyday chores. These include answering the phone, writing e-mail responses to customers, keeping track of orders that keep piling up, providing customer support, organizing his calendar, and scheduling his business travel. In other words, Freddy needs an office assistant. He knows that he cannot afford to hire a full-time employee with a full package of benefits just yet. However, if a temporary employee with hourly pay demonstrates exceptional job skills and an entrepreneurial attitude, Mr. Garcia will consider giving a promotion to a full-time salaried position.

What qualities and qualifications should Mr. Garcia look for in a candidate for the office assistant position? List the top five in the following table and explain why they are important.

Quality or Qualification	Why This Quality or Qualification Is Important
1.	Student answers will vary.
2.	
3.	
4.	
5.	

3. Job Description

Identify a business that you would like to start. Think about the first employee you would need to hire. What would the person's job responsibilities be? In the space provided, write a job description for this position.

JOB DESCRIPTION	
TITLE: _____	
Reports to:	Student answers will vary.
Education:	
Computer experience:	
Job skills:	
Key responsibilities:	
Other characteristics:	

Chapter 14 Human Resources Management

99

Name _____

Communication Activities

4. Safety in the workplace is closely monitored by the Occupational Safety & Health Administration (OSHA), which is a division of the US Department of Labor. Conduct research to find out more about OSHA's regulations for workplace safety. Write an informative report describing your findings. In the space provided, describe how you could implement these regulations in your business.

   Student answers will vary.
   _____
   _____
   _____
   _____
   _____
   _____

5. For many types of businesses, external resources exist to help business owners provide employees with opportunities for professional development. Choose a business that you would like to own. Conduct research to find out what resources are available for professional development for this type of business. List your findings in the space provided. Then prepare an oral report and present your findings to the class.

   Student answers will vary.
   _____
   _____
   _____
   _____
   _____
   _____

6. Conflict resolution is so important in business that many groups provide seminars and other information on how to resolve conflicts. Conduct research to find at least three ways an entrepreneur can increase his or her skill in conflict resolution. List your findings in the space provided. Then write an informative report describing basic conflict resolution principles.

   Student answers will vary.
   _____
   _____
   _____
   _____
   _____
   _____

Copyright Goodheart-Willcox Co., Inc.

CHAPTER 15
Purchases and Inventory Management

Part 1: Check Your Knowledge

Multiple Choice

Write the letter of the correct answer to each question on the line provided.

__C__ 1. The process of buying merchandise for resale to customers is called
   A. sales forecasting.
   B. inventory.
   C. purchasing.
   D. quality control.

__A__ 2. Each of the following steps will help you manage inventory to meet customers' needs, *except*
   A. selling obsolete inventory.
   B. identifying purchasing needs.
   C. studying your market.
   D. identifying vendors.

__D__ 3. The goods and services a company has on hand for resale to customers is its
   A. stockout.
   B. buffer stock.
   C. productive merchandise.
   D. inventory.

__D__ 4. Which of the following is *not* a task associated with inventory management?
   A. Tracking product orders
   B. Organizing products in warehouses
   C. Keeping an adequate assortment of products
   D. Understanding what customers want

__B__ 5. Turnover rate indicates
   A. how quickly invoices are paid.
   B. how quickly merchandise sells.
   C. long-term sales forecasting.
   D. short-term sales forecasting.

__A__ 6. Which of the following is *not* a commonly recognized inventory-control system?
   A. Constant inventory control
   B. Periodic inventory control
   C. Perpetual inventory control
   D. Just-in-time inventory control

__C__ 7. To calculate turnover rate, you need to know
   A. the number of units sold and the monthly supply.
   B. the average number of units on hand and the monthly supply.
   C. the average number of units on hand and the number of units sold.
   D. the productive inventory number and the adequate inventory number.

__B__ 8. Many businesses use the 80/20 rule to
   A. estimate lead time to process an order.
   B. forecast inventory.
   C. calculate monthly supply.
   D. calculate turnover rate.

__A__ 9. To calculate the number of units needed in stock to meet customer demand, you subtract forecasted units from
   A. beginning inventory units.
   B. the monthly inventory.
   C. the productive inventory.
   D. additional units needed in stock.

__B__ 10. The 80/20 rule in inventory forecasting means that
   A. 20% of sales come from 80% of inventory.
   B. 80% of sales come from 20% of inventory.
   C. your turnover rate is 4.
   D. you have 4 months of productive inventory on hand.

True or False

On the line next to each of the following statements, write *True* if the statement is true, or write *False* if the statement is not true.

__True__ 11. Excessive inventory ties up your money so that you cannot use it elsewhere in your business.

__True__ 12. According to the economy of scale concept, producing larger quantities makes the process more efficient, which decreases cost per unit.

__False__ 13. Just-in-time inventory control keeps the maximum amount of inventory on hand to meet an unexpected demand for a product.

__False__ 14. A perpetual inventory-control system is a method of taking a physical count of merchandise at regular intervals.

__True__ 15. The transfer of electronic orders, confirmations, and invoices between businesses is known as electronic data interchange.

__True__ 16. Vendors are companies that sell products to other companies.

__True__ 17. Value is the key to negotiating for quality.

__False__ 18. An invoice is the form a buyer sends to a vendor to officially place an order.

Chapter 15 Purchases and Inventory Management

Name _____

__False__ 19. Product specification is the process of checking goods as they are received to ensure that the quality meets expectations.

__True__ 20. Inventory-risk costs are a form of carrying costs.

Matching

Read the numbered definitions. Then, choose the correct term from the list that follows and write the letter on the line provided next to the definition.

__I__ 21. Running out of stock.

__D__ 22. Document that lists the contents of a box or container.

__B__ 23. Vendor's bill requesting payment for goods shipped or services provided.

__C__ 24. The total time from order placement until the order is received by the customer.

__G__ 25. Form a buyer sends to a vendor to place an order.

__A__ 26. Additional stock kept above the minimum amount required to meet forecasted sales.

__J__ 27. The number of times inventory has been sold during a specific time period.

__F__ 28. Document that describes the size, color, materials, and weight of a product.

__H__ 29. Form on which merchandise received is listed when it arrives at the customer's business.

__E__ 30. An actual count of items in inventory.

A. buffer stock
B. invoice
C. lead time
D. packing slip
E. physical inventory
F. product specification sheet
G. purchase order
H. receiving record
I. stockout
J. turnover rate

Part 2: Activate Your Understanding

Chapter Activities

1. Purchasing Process

    Read each of the following statements and decide which of the eight steps in the purchasing process the statement describes. Write the name of the step in the space provided.

    A. This step involves tracking sales history and performing ongoing sales projections to determine the correct amount of product to keep in inventory.

      Step 1: Identify inventory needs.

B. You may ask colleagues for recommendations, or check references in this step. The Better Business Bureau may offer some helpful information. After you review potential suppliers, you will be ready to take this step.

Step 3: Select the vendor.

C. After identifying a product and a vendor from which to purchase the product, you discuss the price, payment terms, and quality of the product. You may be able to get a quantity discount if you offer to purchase a large number of items.

Step 4: Negotiate the purchase.

D. In this step, you check the contents of the shipment against the packing slip and the purchase order to make sure all the items ordered are included in the shipment.

Step 6: Receive the order.

E. After checking shipments from a vendor, you analyze the reliability of the vendor and the consistency of product quality.

Step 8: Evaluate the vendor.

2. Identifying appropriate vendors is an important part of running a business efficiently. In addition to price—which may vary widely—you must look at quality and at vendor reliability. As the owner of a small office supply store, you are planning to add a line of mechanical pencils to your merchandise. You plan to carry two different brands to provide choices for your customers. Conduct research to find out more about the various brands of mechanical pencils. Choose two brands that would provide a variety for your customers, and find three vendors that carry each brand. (The same vendor may carry both brands.) Record your findings in the table below. Then, in the space provided, identify the vendor or vendors from which you would order the pencils.

Brand	Vendor	Price

Vendor or vendors selected: _____

Reasons: Student answers will vary. Major brands include BIC®, Alvin™, Pilot®, PaperMate®, Pentel®, and Sanford®. Prices vary by vendor and by the intended use of the pencil. To provide a variety of choices, students may choose Alvin drafting pencils and a less expensive mechanical pencil, such as BIC or PaperMate.

Chapter 15 Purchases and Inventory Management

Name _____

Communication Activities

3. A business friend in another city has sent you an e-mail message. She says she has heard about the benefits of the JIT inventory-control system, but she is not sure whether this method will work well for her small business. Write a three- or four-paragraph business e-mail to your friend explaining what the JIT system is and how it can benefit her small business. Be sure to use correct business e-mail etiquette. In the space provided, write a sentence summarizing the information in your e-mail message.

   Student answers will vary.

   _____

   _____

   _____

4. RFID devices are now used in many different applications. Conduct research to find out more about these devices and their current uses. Write an informative report describing the various ways in which RFID technology can benefit a business. In the space provided, list the sources you used to create the report.

   Student answers will vary. RFID devices are currently being used in inventory systems and

   product tracking, as well as in managing the transportation and distribution of products. RFID

   technology also allows customers to make payments using a smartphone. Individual industries

   also have industry-specific uses for RFIDs.

Math Activities

5. Last summer, your friend Bill started his own business of producing T-shirts with individualized logos and prints. His business took off quickly and proved to be successful. However, he has run into some order fulfillment problems, and he does not want to disappoint his customers due to insufficient stock. At the same time, he cannot afford to invest a lot of money in inventory. His current inventory is 1300 T-shirts. Bill realizes that this may be not enough to meet future sales. He recorded his monthly T-shirt sales during the last year (see the table below), and he believes that his sales for the next year will remain the same. Calculate the minimum number of additional T-shirts needed in stock, if any, to meet last year's sales numbers. *Hint:* Use Bill's current inventory as the beginning inventory and use the formula given in the chapter.

	Jan.	Feb.	Mar.	Apr.	May	June	July	Aug.	Sep.	Oct.	Nov.	Dec.
T-shirts	100	120	120	120	120	120	150	150	150	150	200	200

Total sales during the previous year (forecasted sales): 1700

Number of additional T-shirts needed: 1700 − 1300 = 400 shirts needed

6. Calculate the turnover rate for each of the following businesses. Round your answers to the nearest tenth.

   A. A stationery supply store has a cost of goods sold of $85,000 for the previous year. The average inventory on hand at the end of the year was $25,000.

   Turnover rate: $85,000 ÷ $25,000 = 3.4 times

   B. A local department store had an inventory of $264,000 at the beginning of the previous year. During the year, the store purchased additional inventory totaling $103,000. The ending inventory was $152,000, and the average inventory on hand at the end of the year was $156,000.

   Turnover rate: ($264,000 + $103,000 − 152,000) ÷ $156,000 = 1.4 times

   C. A convenience store has a cost of goods sold of $195,000 for the previous year. The average inventory on hand at the end of the year was $89,000.

   Turnover rate: $195,000 ÷ $89,000 = 2.2 times

Name _____ Date _____ Period _____

CHAPTER 16
Risk Management

Part 1: Check Your Knowledge

Multiple Choice

Write the letter of the correct answer to each question on the line provided.

__A__ 1. The process of identifying risks that apply to your business and planning how to handle them is called
   A. risk management.
   B. economic planning.
   C. insurable interest.
   D. business management.

__D__ 2. All risks can be classified as either speculative or
   A. natural.
   B. controllable.
   C. human.
   D. pure.

__D__ 3. An uninsurable risk is one that
   A. cannot be predicted.
   B. cannot be avoided.
   C. is caused by nature.
   D. an insurance company will not cover.

__B__ 4. Malware is a(n)
   A. theft that does not involve the use of force or violence.
   B. program intended to destroy or steal data from a computer.
   C. act of cheating a business out of money or property.
   D. act of breaking into a business to steal merchandise or money.

__C__ 5. Shoplifting is a type of
   A. natural risk.
   B. market risk.
   C. human risk.
   D. economic risk.

Copyright Goodheart-Willcox Co., Inc.   107

__A__ 6. Embezzlement is a form of
   A. fraud.
   B. burglary.
   C. robbery.
   D. shoplifting.

__B__ 7. An electronic tag on merchandise that sets off an alarm if it is removed from the store is an example of a
   A. surveillance system.
   B. theft deterrent.
   C. security policy.
   D. safety program.

__C__ 8. Which government organization enforces safety regulations in the workplace?
   A. NOCTI
   B. CDC
   C. OSHA
   D. FDA

__D__ 9. The type of insurance that provides medical and financial support for workers who are injured on the job is
   A. business owner's policy insurance.
   B. corporate insurance.
   C. employee health insurance.
   D. worker's compensation.

__B__ 10. An agreement that promises to give customers their money back if a product is faulty is a(n)
   A. warranty.
   B. guarantee.
   C. insurance policy.
   D. surety bond.

True or False

On the line next to each of the following statements, write *True* if the statement is true, or write *False* if the statement is not true.

__False__ 11. The term *shrinkage* refers to inventory loss caused by natural causes such as tornados.

__True__ 12. A business that chooses to self-insure is responsible for 100 percent of the risk.

__True__ 13. Political risk is greatest for companies that do business with foreign countries that do *not* have a free trade agreement with the US.

__False__ 14. An individual who owes money for goods or services received is called a creditor.

__False__ 15. Secured loans do *not* require collateral.

__True__ 16. Companies that allow customers to pay for their purchases in several installments should use a credit application to check the customers' financial backgrounds.

Chapter 16 Risk Management

Name _____

__False__ 17. A surety bond is a record of a company's credit history and financial behavior.

__False__ 18. The three Cs of credit are character, capacity, and contract.

__True__ 19. An aging report shows how long accounts have remained unpaid.

__True__ 20. Strong passwords and firewalls are examples of data security measures.

Matching

Read the numbered definitions. Then, choose the correct term from the list that follows and write the letter on the line provided next to the definition.

__E__ 21. Cheating or deceiving a business out of money or property.

__J__ 22. A promise to replace or repair faulty products.

__A__ 23. Breaking into a business to steal money, merchandise, or confidential information.

__D__ 24. Someone trusted with confidential information, financial records, money, or other valuables takes it for personal gain.

__H__ 25. Someone who takes goods from a store without paying for them.

__B__ 26. A private firm that maintains consumer credit data and provides information to businesses for a fee.

__I__ 27. A three-party contract that guarantees that one party will fulfill its obligations to a second party.

__G__ 28. Theft involving another person, often through the use of force or violence.

__C__ 29. A record of a company or person's credit history and financial behavior.

__F__ 30. A promise to refund money paid for a faulty product.

A. burglary
B. credit bureau
C. credit report
D. embezzlement
E. fraud
F. guarantee
G. robbery
H. shoplifter
I. surety bond
J. warranty

Part 2: Activate Your Understanding

Chapter Activities

1. Analyzing Risks

    Choose a type of business that you would like to own and write it in the space provided. Think about the risks to which this business may be exposed. Record examples of each type of business risk in the table below. Decide whether you can anticipate, prepare for, or recover from each example you have listed. If so, explain how you would do so.

    Type of business: _____

Type of Risk	Examples	Controllable? If Yes, How?
Natural Risks		
Student answers will vary.		
Human Risks		
Economic and Political Risks		
Market Risks		

Chapter 16 Risk Management

Name _____

2. Market Risks

Conduct research to find a product that has been very successful in the last few years, and one that has not been successful. Complete the table below by listing the products, describing the product features, and providing a possible reason for the product's success or failure. In the space provided below the table, write a general statement about the characteristics of a successful product.

	Product Name	**Description of Features**	**Reason for Success or Failure**
Successful Product			
Unsuccessful Product			

Student answers will vary.

Communication Activities

3. Develop a list of five questions that are critical to the issue of risk management. In your questions, use the vocabulary from this chapter correctly. Record your questions in the space provided. Then facilitate a class discussion using one of your questions as a springboard. Encourage as many classmates as possible to participate in the discussion.

   Question 1: _____
   Student answers will vary.
   _____

   Question 2: _____
   _____
   _____

   Question 3: _____
   _____
   _____

   Question 4: _____
   _____
   _____

   Question 5: _____
   _____
   _____

4. Choose a natural disaster that has struck the United States sometime within the last 50 years. Conduct research to find out more about the effect of the disaster on businesses in the area. Write an informative report describing your findings. In the space provided, record the resources you used to prepare the report.

   Student answers will vary.
   _____
   _____
   _____
   _____

5. A business owner who accepts counterfeit money loses both the money and the product for which the counterfeit money was paid. Conduct research to find out how to detect counterfeit money. Create an oral report of your findings. Record your sources in the space provided.

   Student answers will vary. The US Secret Service has a website dedicated to educating the

   public on how to identify counterfeit money, and many other websites offer further tips.
   _____
   _____

Chapter 16   Risk Management

Name _____

6. Conduct research to find out more about credit bureaus and credit reports. Write an informative report about your findings. Include the answers to the questions below in your report.

   A. What are the three main credit bureaus in the United States?

   Experian®, Transunion®, and Equifax®

   B. What types of information are included in a credit report?

   Credit reports contain information about a person's current and previous residences, employment history, credit and credit payment history, whether accounts are current, closed, or delinquent, and unpaid balances, among other information. Credit reports also contain the person's date of birth and social security number.

   C. How can a company's credit report affect the business?

   Student answers will vary, but students may find that a better credit rating can help a company get better interest rates on business loans and insurance.

Name _____ Date _____ Period _____

Financial Management

Part 1: Check Your Knowledge

Multiple Choice

Write the letter of the correct answer to each question on the line provided.

__B__ 1. Because the accounting process is an established standard for communicating financial information, it is often called the
   A. business standard.
   B. language of business.
   C. financial language.
   D. financial standard.

__A__ 2. The two accepted accounting methods are the accrual basis and the
   A. cash basis.
   B. flexible basis.
   C. credit basis.
   D. double-entry basis.

__C__ 3. The system of recording business transactions, analyzing them, and reporting the results is called
   A. posting.
   B. journalizing.
   C. accounting.
   D. reconciling.

__B__ 4. The fiscal period used by most businesses is
   A. one month.
   B. one year.
   C. one quarter.
   D. six months.

__D__ 5. Business records should be kept
   A. in secret.
   B. available to anyone who wants to view them.
   C. together with personal records.
   D. separately from personal records.

__A__ 6. Which of the following is *not* a type of special journal?
   A. General journal
   B. Cash receipts journal
   C. Cash payments journal
   D. Sales journal

__D__ 7. Double-entry accounting is the process of
   A. using the accounting equation to record information.
   B. listing liabilities and assets.
   C. recording business transactions in a journal and in a ledger.
   D. recording the debit and credit parts of a transaction.

__C__ 8. A stakeholder is someone who
   A. audits federal taxes for a business.
   B. prepares the financial reports for a business.
   C. has an interest in a business.
   D. carries out negotiations for a business.

__B__ 9. A cash flow statement reports how cash
   A. moves from investors into a business.
   B. moves into and out of a business.
   C. is recorded in the balance sheet.
   D. is recorded in financial statements.

__D__ 10. A positive cash flow results when
   A. assets are greater than liabilities.
   B. accounts payable are less than accounts receivable.
   C. the business spends the same amount of cash it receives.
   D. the business receives more cash than it spends.

True or False

On the line next to each of the following statements, write *True* if the statement is true, or write *False* if the statement is not true.

__True__ 11. Operating ratio shows the relationship of expenses to sales.

__True__ 12. Financial ratios are used to evaluate a company's overall financial condition.

__False__ 13. Working capital is the amount of money a business has to pay in wages to hired workers.

__False__ 14. Owner's equity statements report how much money the business owner owes in taxes.

__True__ 15. The profit and loss (P & L) statement is also known as an income statement.

__False__ 16. The balance sheet reports the net income or net loss of a business.

__True__ 17. A group of accounts is collectively known as the general ledger.

__True__ 18. Individual accounts for customers and vendors are called *subsidiary ledgers*.

Chapter 17 Financial Management **117**

Name _____

__True__ 19. Liability is anything that is owed by the business.

__False__ 20. Accounts payable are considered assets.

Matching

Read the numbered definitions. Then, choose the correct term from the list that follows and write the letter on the line provided next to the definition.

__B__ 21. An organization that exists independently of the owner's personal finances.

__D__ 22. The period of time for which a business summarizes accounting information and prepares financial statements.

__H__ 23. A transaction for which merchandise purchased will be paid to the vendor at a later date.

__E__ 24. Generally accepted accounting principles.

__C__ 25. A method of accounting that recognizes revenue when it is received and expenses when they are paid.

__F__ 26. A document that reports the revenue and expenses of a business for a specific time period and shows a net income or loss.

__A__ 27. A method of accounting in which revenues and expenses are recorded when they occur.

__J__ 28. The amount of money a business has after the liabilities are paid.

__G__ 29. The transferring of information from journals to the ledger.

__I__ 30. A transaction for which cash for the sale will be received at a later date.

A. accrual basis
B. business entity
C. cash basis
D. fiscal period
E. GAAP
F. income statement
G. posting
H. purchase on account
I. sale on account
J. working capital

Part 2: Activate Your Understanding

Chapter Activities

1. Balance Sheet

   A balance sheet reports the assets, liabilities, and owner's equity. To prepare a balance sheet correctly, you must understand which items are considered assets and which are liabilities. The following list shows the figures from a Whitfield Vegetable Harvest on December 31, 20__. Select each item from the list and place it in the appropriate column in the table below. Calculate the company's total assets, total liabilities, and owner's equity based on these figures.

Cash	$18,000
Accounts Payable	$12,000
Accounts Receivable	$11,000
Equipment	$15,000
Notes Payable	$20,000

Assets		Liabilities	
Cash	$18,000	Accounts Payable	$12,000
Accounts Receivable	$11,000	Notes Payable	$20,000
Equipment	$15,000		
Total Assets:	**$44,000**	**Total Liabilities:**	**$32,000**

   Owner's Equity: _Owner's Equity: $44,000 − $32,000 = $12,000_

2. Analyzing a Balance Sheet

   The balance sheet is a snapshot of the financial health of a business. Using the information from activity 1, answer the following questions.

   A. What is the financial condition of Whitfield Vegetable Harvest on December 31, 20__?

   Student answers will vary.

   B. What do you think the lenders will say about Whitfield's ability to repay the outstanding loan?

   Student answers will vary.

Chapter 17 Financial Management

Name _____

3. Accounting Services

   A. List the pros and cons of hiring a professional to provide accounting services to your business.

   Pros:

   Student answers will vary.
   _____
   _____
   _____

   Cons:
   _____
   _____
   _____
   _____

   B. Select two specific tasks that an accountant typically performs and record these tasks in the table. Briefly explain why these tasks are significant for your business, your investors, and the Internal Revenue Service (IRS).

Significance for:	Task 1	Task 2
	Student answers will vary.	
Your Business		
Your Investors		
IRS		

Communication Activities

4. Importance of Financial Statements

   Conduct research to find out more about financial statements. Write an informative report describing the importance of financial statements for an entrepreneur. Explain what conclusions the stakeholders may draw from the entrepreneur's financial statements. In the space provided, list the resources you used to prepare your report.

   Student answers will vary.

5. Conduct research to find out more about the practical effects of using the cash basis or accrual basis of accounting. In your opinion, is one method better than another for the majority of small businesses? Prepare a persuasive speech to convince your classmates to agree. In the space provided, list the main points you will cover in your speech.

   Student answers will vary.

Math Activities

Calculate the answer to each of the following questions. Round your answers to the nearest hundredth, when applicable.

6. Company A's current total assets are $87,000, and its current liabilities equal $49,000.

   A. How much working capital does Company A have?

   $87,000 − $49,000 = $38,000

   B. What is Company A's current ratio?

   $87,000 ÷ $49,000 = 1.78:1

   C. What is Company A's debt ratio?

   $49,000 ÷ $87,000 = .56:1

7. Company B's total sales equal $186,000, and its net income is $109,000. The company's total expenses are $74,500.

   A. What is Company B's net profit ratio?

   $109,000 ÷ $186,000 = .59:1

   B. What is Company B's operating ratio?

   $74,500 ÷ $186,000 = .40:1

CHAPTER 18: Business Growth

Part 1: Check Your Knowledge

Multiple Choice

Write the letter of the correct answer to each question on the line provided.

__A__ 1. An economic situation in which a country experiences negative economic growth for a period of six months or longer is a
   A. recession.
   B. depression.
   C. contraction.
   D. trough.

__A__ 2. Which of the following is *not* a reason why growing your business during an economic downturn is considered a good idea?
   A. Market penetration is only possible during an economic downturn.
   B. It provides an opportunity to hire better-qualified people.
   C. Obtaining credit is easier during an economic downturn.
   D. Land, equipment, supplies, and buildings may be cheaper.

__B__ 3. Organic growth is growth that is accomplished by
   A. merging with another company.
   B. expanding the current business.
   C. increasing the sales of organic food.
   D. buying another business.

__C__ 4. Intensive growth strategies are ways of growing your business by
   A. attempting synergistic diversification.
   B. merging with another company.
   C. taking advantage of opportunities in your current market.
   D. buying a product for your line.

__D__ 5. For a beauty salon, adding which of the following products or services is an example of synergistic diversification?
   A. Selling magazines
   B. Having a photographer on staff to take pictures of patrons
   C. Selling refreshments
   D. Selling hair styling products

__D__ 6. Market penetration
   A. is associated with organic growth.
   B. does not involve increased sales.
   C. is another name for franchising.
   D. is an intensive growth strategy.

__B__ 7. Market penetration methods may include
   A. convincing customers to shop on weekends.
   B. increasing advertising and promotion.
   C. increasing prices.
   D. restricting shopping hours.

__B__ 8. Intensive growth strategies include all of the following *except*
   A. market penetration.
   B. backward integration.
   C. market development.
   D. product development.

__C__ 9. One role of the Small Business Administration is to
   A. loan money to established businesses.
   B. loan money to unknown businesses.
   C. guarantee loans made by banks and other loan institutions.
   D. complete all the required paperwork for small businesses.

__B__ 10. The Small Business Investment Company (SBIC)
   A. is a public investor.
   B. receives matching funding from the SBA.
   C. receives funding from private investors.
   D. is licensed and regulated by the Federal Reserve.

True or False

On the line next to each of the following statements, write *True* if the statement is true, or write *False* if the statement is not true.

__True__ 11. Market penetration is associated with increasing sales in the existing target market.

__False__ 12. Organic growth may be accomplished through buying another business or merging with another company.

__True__ 13. Diversification involves adding products, services, locations, customers, or markets.

__True__ 14. Horizontal diversification is adding new products that are not related to your current product line.

__False__ 15. Forward integration occurs when you buy one of your vendors.

__True__ 16. Rapid business expansion is typical for the growth phase of the business cycle.

__True__ 17. Venture capitalists are one source of equity financing for a business owner.

__False__ 18. Trade credit requires a business to pay for products received before it resells them.

Chapter 18   Business Growth

Name _____

__False__ 19. The lowest point of the business cycle is the contraction phase.

__False__ 20. Markup is the increase in the price of goods and services over time.

Matching

Read the numbered definitions. Then, choose the correct term from the list that follows and write the letter on the line provided next to the definition.

__G__ 21. Two companies agree to combine as a new company.

__I__ 22. Profits put aside from the operation of the company that can be used for expansion.

__A__ 23. One company purchases another company.

__D__ 24. Adding new products to your company that are not related to your current product line.

__E__ 25. Negative economic growth for at least a six-month period.

__B__ 26. A company buys one of its vendors.

__H__ 27. Negative economic growth for at least a six-month period.

__F__ 28. The first time shares of stock are available for public purchase.

__J__ 29. Adding new product lines or businesses that are compatible with yours.

__C__ 30. A company buys a business for which it serves as a vendor.

A. acquisition
B. backward integration
C. forward integration
D. horizontal diversification
E. inflation
F. initial public offering
G. merger
H. recession
I. retained earnings
J. synergistic diversification

Part 2: Activate Your Understanding

Chapter Activities

1. Financing Business Growth

    Business growth can be financed using equity financing or bank loans, or by becoming a public corporation by issuing an IPO. In the space provided, record the nature of your business. Then complete the table to identify the advantages and disadvantages of each method for financing growth in your business. Compare the advantages and disadvantages, and decide which type of financing would be most appropriate for your business growth. Write your conclusions in the space provided below the table.

    Your business: _____

	Advantages	Disadvantages
Equity Financing	Student answers will vary.	
Bank Loans		
IPO		

    Your conclusions: _____

    _____

    _____

2. Organic Growth

    Think about ways you can grow the business you identified in activity 1. Complete the table below to identify specific methods of organic growth for your business. Provide at least four examples for each strategy.

	Market Penetration	Market Development
Method 1	Student answers will vary, but should include at least some of the organic growth strategies described in the chapter.	
Method 2		
Method 3		
Method 4		

Chapter 18 Business Growth

Name _____

3. Diversification

For each type of business listed in the table below, list one synergistic diversification and one horizontal diversification that might help the business grow.

Business Type	Synergistic Diversification	Horizontal Diversification
Car rental agency	Student answers will vary.	
Coffee shop		
Clothing specialty shop		
Auto parts store		
Computer repair shop		
Grocery store		

Communication Activities

4. When two companies agree to merge, the merger is generally intended to expand the business. This may or may not happen, however. Conduct research to find at least two specific examples of major companies that have merged in the last 20 years. Write an informative report describing the companies that merged and how the merger affected the growth of the merged company. In the space provided, record the sources you used to create your report.

    Student answers will vary.

5. Conduct research to find out more about the Farm Service Agency. What types of assistance does the FSA offer to farmers, ranchers, and other agricultural businesses? Write an informative report describing the information you find. Include specific information about farm loan programs offered by the FSA. In the space provided, write a summary sentence explaining how the FSA helps US businesses grow.

    Student answers will vary. The FSA provides farm operating loans, farm ownership loans, emergency loans, and loans to minority and women farmers and ranchers. It also provides loans for people who are new to agriculture (beginning farmers and ranchers) and works with rural youth programs such as 4-H, FFA, and Youth Farmers to provide loans to individual youths.

6. Conduct research to find out more about the World Bank Group. In the space provided, list the five agencies that make up the World Bank Group. Then prepare an oral report describing how the projects currently underway can help entrepreneurs and small businesses in the United States.

The five agencies that make up the World Bank Group are the International Bank for Reconstruction and Development (IBRD), the International Development Association (IDA), the International Finance Corporation (IFC), the Multilateral Investment Guarantee Agency (MIGA), and the International Centre for Settlement of Investment Disputes (ICSID). Student oral reports will vary.

CHAPTER 19 Exit Strategies

Part 1: Check Your Knowledge

Multiple Choice

Write the letter of the correct answer to each question on the line provided.

__C__ 1. Passing a business on to the owner's children would be called a(n)
   A. working plan.
   B. liquidation.
   C. exit strategy.
   D. conflict of interest.

__B__ 2. All of the following are considered exiting the business *except*
   A. taking the company public.
   B. expanding the business.
   C. liquidating the business.
   D. ending a brand.

__C__ 3. Which type of plan details who will run the company in the event the owner dies, retires, or leaves the company for any other reason?
   A. Business plan
   B. Tactical plan
   C. Succession plan
   D. Working plan

__A__ 4. A legally binding agreement that allows the owner to sell all or part of his or her interest in the company is known as a(n)
   A. buy-sell agreement.
   B. acquisition agreement.
   C. exit agreement.
   D. industrial agreement.

__D__ 5. A plan that calls for extracting cash from a business, brand, or product line is known as a(n)
   A. exchange plan.
   B. business plan.
   C. strategic plan.
   D. harvest strategy.

__A__ 6. A transaction in which a business is sold in full and the ownership is transferred immediately is a(n)
   A. outright sale.
   B. gradual sale.
   C. lease agreement.
   D. indirect sale.

__C__ 7. The most common form of employee ownership is the
   A. outright sale.
   B. lease program.
   C. employee stock option plan.
   D. buyout agreement.

__B__ 8. A contract that provides a person with temporary rights to the business and details the conditions and payments the owner receives in return is a(n)
   A. employee stock option plan.
   B. lease.
   C. buyout agreement.
   D. gradual sales plan.

__C__ 9. A merger is one way of
   A. leasing a company.
   B. liquidating a company.
   C. transferring company ownership.
   D. taking a company public.

__D__ 10. According to the Workers Adjustment and Retraining Notification Act (WARN), how much notice must employees be given that the company is going to close?
   A. 15 days
   B. 30 days
   C. 45 days
   D. 60 days

True or False

On the line next to each of the following statements, write *True* if the statement is true, or write *False* if the statement is not true.

__False__ 11. Mergers are not considered an exit strategy.

__False__ 12. The most common form of employee ownership is a buy-sell agreement.

__True__ 13. When the new owner finances the purchase with a long-term payment plan, making payments to the seller, while the seller transitions out of the business, this is known as a gradual sale.

__True__ 14. A harvest strategy is a way to repay investors while providing an exit for the owner.

__True__ 15. Transferring ownership to a family member can have both emotional and economic impacts.

__True__ 16. Buy-sell agreements are sometimes called *buyout agreements*.

__False__ 17. A succession plan describes the organizational structure of a family-run business.

Chapter 19 Exit Strategies

Name _____

__True____ 18. An advantage to the lessee in a lease agreement is being able to run the business with the expertise and advice of the owner.

__False___ 19. Once a business is closed, taxes owed are no longer collectible.

__True____ 20. An ESOP can be set up for both privately and publicly held companies.

Matching

Read the numbered definitions. Then, choose the correct term from the list that follows and write the letter on the line provided next to the definition.

__G__ 21. A contract that provides an individual with temporary rights to a business.

__B__ 22. A legally binding contract that controls when an owner can sell interest in the partnership of the business.

__I__ 23. The business is sold in full and ownership is transferred immediately.

__F__ 24. A planned method for extracting cash from a business, brand, or product.

__J__ 25. A plan that details what will happen in the event the owner leaves the business.

__C__ 26. The employer sells the company to the employees.

__H__ 27. The sale of all assets of a business, including equipment and buildings.

__D__ 28. A trust fund set up to contribute new shares or cash to purchase existing shares on behalf of the employees.

__A__ 29. An outright purchase of one business by another business.

__E__ 30. The new owner finances the purchase with a long-term payment plan.

A. acquisition
B. buy-sell agreement
C. EBO
D. ESOP
E. gradual sale
F. harvest strategy
G. lease agreement
H. liquidation
I. outright sale
J. succession plan

Part 2: Activate Your Understanding

Chapter Activities

1. Buy-Sell Agreements

    Choose two small businesses in your area and contact the owner(s) to see if they have a buy-sell agreement or succession plan in place. In the space provided, record the names of the businesses and the industry they are in (for example, retail). Describe how they came to the agreement if they have one in place, or what their plans may be to put one in place.

    Company 1: _Student answers will vary._

    Company 2: _____

2. Employee Stock Options

    Conduct research in your area to find a company that has an employee stock option plan. List five questions you would ask the owners of the business regarding their decisions for using the ESOP method. Ask the questions to the owners and analyze the responses. Record your findings in the space provided.

    Business name: _Student answers will vary._

    Questions:

    1. _____
    2. _____
    3. _____
    4. _____
    5. _____

Chapter 19 Exit Strategies **131**

Name _____

Analysis of responses: _____

_____

_____

_____

_____

_____

_____

3. Going Out of Business/Liquidation

   In tough economic times, it is not hard to find businesses that are going out of business. Identify a business in your area and list four questions you would like to ask the owners about the reasons they are exiting the business. List the questions below. Then conduct an interview with the owners to ask your questions. Summarize your findings in the space provided.

   Question 1: _Student answers will vary._

   _____

   Answer to Question 1: _____

   _____

   _____

   Question 2: _____

   _____

   Answer to Question 2: _____

   _____

   _____

   Question 3: _____

   _____

   Answer to Question 3: _____

   _____

   _____

   Question 4: _____

   _____

   Answer to Question 4: _____

   _____

   _____

Analysis and Summary: _____

_____

_____

_____

_____

_____

4. Exiting Experts

   When a business owner considers exiting a business, he or she can consult a number of different kinds of experts. Conduct research to determine the average fees charged by the following experts in your area for assisting with a harvest plan. Find out what additional information would be necessary for a business owner to make a wise decision with the exit strategy. Record your findings in the table below.

Expert	Fee Charged	Information Needed
Attorney		Student answers will vary.
Accountant		
Banker		
Internal Revenue Service		

Communication Activities

5. The IPO process can be fairly involved, especially when the company is large. Even for small businesses, however, the process must be well planned in advance if it is to succeed. Conduct research to find out more about the process of preparing for and executing an initial public offering. Write an informative report about your findings. Use the following questions as a guide for your report.

   A. What are some of the reasons a company may want to go public?

   Student answers will vary. Examples include owner retirement, getting access to capital

   markets to raise money for expansion, diversification, and attract talented employees.

   _____

   _____

   _____

Chapter 19 Exit Strategies

Name _____

B. How do current market conditions affect a potential IPO?

Student answers will vary. Market conditions have an impact on the valuation of the

company, which affects the price of the initial stock offering.

C. What are some of the pros and cons of taking a company public?

Student answers will vary. Pros may include increased cash availability, new opportunities

for growth, improved reputation, and increased market value. Cons may include increased

expenses and vulnerability to acquisition by hostile takeover.